Boldly beloved

ASHLEY DJOKOTO

Boldly Beloved
Copyright © 2024 Ashley Djokoto

All rights reserved. This book is protected by copyright laws of the United States of America. This book may not be copied or reprinted for commercial gain or profit.

Unless otherwise stated, Scripture quotations are from the ESV® Bible (The Holy Bible, English Standard Version®), © 2001 by Crossway, a publishing ministry of Good News Publishers. Used by permission. All rights reserved. The ESV text may not be quoted in any publication made available to the public by a Creative Commons license. The ESV may not be translated in whole or in part into any other language.

Cover & Interior Design by Milk & Honey Books, LLC

ISBN 13 TP: 978-1-953000-38-5
ISBN 13 eBook: 978-1-953000-39-2

Dedication

This book is dedicated to: The young women I've had the joy of teaching and discipling — I wrote these words with you in mind; And to my husband, who is my biggest cheerleader and my best friend.

Table of Contents

Introduction | 6

Part I: I am loved | 9
I am loved
I am accepted
I am treasured
I am adored
I am remembered

Part II: I am created | 23
I am created
I am the image of God
I am a masterpiece
I am beautiful
I am uniquely me

Part III: I am saved | 37
I am saved
I am forgiven
I am redeemed
I am restored
I am a new creation

Part IV: I am made righteous | 51
I am made righteous
I am justified
I am delivered
I am faith-filled
I am clothed in righteousness

**Part V:
I am being made like Christ | 65**
I am being made like Christ
I am Spirit-led

I am dead to self
I am a temple
I am holy

Part VI: I am a good thing | 79
I am a good thing
I am being made beautiful
I am whole
I am pure
I am godly

Part VII: I am adopted | 93
I am adopted
I am chosen
I am grafted in
I am safe
I am one who lacks nothing

Part VIII: I am anointed | 107
I am anointed
I am equipped
I am purposed
I am salt & light
I am a builder

Part IX: I am appointed | 121
I am appointed
I am a living sacrifice
I am part of a chosen people
I am part of a royal priesthood
I am part of a holy nation

Part X: I am called | 135
I am called

I am kept
I am created for a purpose
I am created for good works
I am fruitful

Part XI: I am gifted | 149
I am gifted
I am a creator
I am an encourager
I am a helpmate
I am a watch[woman]

Part XII: I am surrendered | 165
I am surrendered
I am a servant
I am humble
I am kind
I am content

Part XIII: I am a witness | 181
I am a witness
I am full of love
I am created to love
I am a gardener
I am an ambassador

**Part XIV:
I am created for relationships | 197**
I am created for relationships
I am a daughter
I am a sister
I am a friend
I am a bridge

Part XV: I am the Church | 209
I am the Church
I am the Bride
I am the Body
I am beloved
I am united

Part XVI: I am blessed | 225
I am blessed
I am highly favored
I am the head
I am confident
I am valued

Part XVII: I am an overcomer | 239
I am an overcomer
I am strong
I am full of endurance
I am courageous
I am a conqueror

Part XVIII: I am worth it | 253
I am worth it
I am free
I am sent
I am victorious
I am heaven-bound

About the Author | 268
Endnotes | 269

Introduction

You've probably heard that God loves you before. Every Sunday school lesson, youth group retreat, and worship song we sing in church tells us this fact. But how many of us actually believe it? How many of us *live* like we know God loves us? This devotional is for any young woman who struggles to believe God really, really does love her. Despite your shortcomings. Despite your failures. Despite your weaknesses. The God of the Universe created you and said, "Wow. That one is *good*." He chose you. He made you with a purpose. He loves you. He has called you his beloved.

Don't believe me yet? That's okay; it took me a while, too. Sometimes I still have a tough time with it. I suppose that's the way we're hardwired—to compare God's love with man's love and somehow think that if people's love for us is broken, then God's love must be the same. But that's not what the Bible tells us. God's handwritten letter to us tells a vastly different story. It tells of God's great, astounding love for people of every nature and nation. It tells us of His great, astonishing plan for mankind. And it tells how we broke it, stomped on His plan, threw His love to the ground, and walked away. But then it tells of His redeeming love, the love that came into the world as a man and sacrificed Himself so we could be redeemed, too.

Friend, I'd love for you to keep reading about this amazing, astounding, abiding love. This love that changes lives. It changed my life, and it can change yours, too.

With love, your friend & sister in Christ,

Ashley

How This Devotional is Set Up

In each day's devotional, you'll read an I AM statement. I chose to write it this way based on Moses' encounter with God in Exodus 3 when God tells Moses His name is "I AM." Genesis 2 tells us that we are made in God's image, therefore we are made in the I AM's image. We are the exact image of God, except sin has marred us and made us broken, so we don't always reflect Him the way we should. **This devotional is to encourage you to claim who you were created to be in Christ, to internalize His promises for you, and to reflect His image to the world around you.**

Each day, there will be multiple verses to read and reflect on, as well as a challenge and a prayer. I would encourage you to read the verses and their context in your Bible, not just in this book. Don't believe everything I write without investigating God's Word for yourself. The daily challenges are for you to put into practice what the I AM statement of the day is. The prayer is a guide to what you can say to God, but please add your own words. My prayer is by the end of these ninety days, you'll be more comfortable talking to God and reading His Word. And most importantly, you'll be able to "grasp how wide and how long and how high and how deep the love of Christ is" (Ephesians 3:18 ESV).

So, start reading, sister. Let's jump into the love of God together. Let His Word permeate your heart, His Spirit take control. Doing life God's way brings joy, peace, and everlasting love. He made you for a reason; He loves you and will never forsake you. He can be your best friend, and He will walk with you every step of the way.

Part I

I am loved

"For God so loved the world that He gave His only Son"

John 3:16

I am loved

"For God so loved the world that He gave His only Son, that whoever believes in Him has eternal life."
John 3:16

What does it mean to be loved? Every human will ask themselves this question at one point. Does it mean to get butterflies in your stomach when a cute guy talks to you? Does it mean to tell someone you love them? Does it mean to give up something meaningful for someone else?

Love is more than words or feelings. Love is the action of putting others above yourself. Scripture tells us "God is love" (1 John 4:8). God is love because He created love, defines love, and represents the epitome of love when He sent His Son as a sacrifice for you and me to be welcomed into His family.

This is big. You are *loved* by the Most High God. The Creator of the Universe loves you. He created everything in the earth, under the earth, and in the sea, and He sees you and loves you. In fact, He loves you so much that before the beginning of time, He chose to send His only Son to die for you. He did all this to make you holy and pure in His sight.

"Even as He chose us in [Christ] before the foundation of the world, that we should be holy and blameless before Him. In love, He predestined us for adoption to Himself as [daughters] through Jesus Christ." Ephesians 1:4-5

No matter what you've been through or what you believe about yourself, you are loved. Deeply and irrevocably. This love is far greater than that which any man, friend, or parent could show you. God sees every part of you and loves you the same. This is eternal and unconditional love. It is unchanging and everlasting love.

Challenge: There's power when you speak the truth to yourself aloud. I had very low self-esteem growing up, and I had to fight self-destructive and insecure thoughts about myself often. One way I learned to fight these thoughts was through learning what God's Word says and speaking it to myself when those negative thoughts came my way. I'd encourage you to do the same. Say His Word out loud every day. Write it on your bathroom mirror, your locker at school, or on the dashboard of your car. Remember it. Meditate on it. Pray it. His Word will change you little by little.

Prayer: Thank You, Jesus, for loving me. Thank You for dying on the cross and going through such pain so I could be made right with You and spend eternity with You. Thank You for loving me with everlasting and steadfast love. I love You. Amen.

I am accepted

"Therefore welcome one another as Christ has welcomed you, for the glory of God."
—Romans 15:7

Have you ever felt left out of something, like you didn't quite make the cut? Or have you experienced the genuine anxiety of FOMO – fear of missing out?

I grew up always wishing I were like someone else. You may have similar thoughts about yourself. Being one of the tallest girls in my high school of over four thousand people didn't help my desire to fit in and not stand out. I had a deep desire to be accepted by my peers, my teachers, my friends, and my parents. In my head, I didn't think I was, and it created a lot of anxiety for me.One of my youth pastors showed me this verse in Zephaniah, and it slowly but surely changed my way of thinking.

"The Lord your God is in your midst, a mighty one who will save; He will rejoice over you with gladness; He will quiet you with His love; He will exult over you with loud singing."
—Zephaniah 3:17

God, the creator of the whole universe, delights in you. He sings over you. Not only sings but rejoices and exults over you. He rejoices that you are you. He created you for a reason. Whatever you don't like about yourself right now, trust that God has a purpose for it. He accepts you, one hundred percent of you, just as you are. He even sent His only Son to die for you before you could do anything for Him That's the kind of love and acceptance God has for us.

Challenge: List ten things about yourself that you love. Then think of those things you'd rather change. Spend time thanking God for both lists.

Prayer: Thank You, Jesus, for accepting me. Not just accepting me but dying for me. Thank You for Your Word that tells me you sing and rejoice over me. Remind me of this truth daily. Thank You for Your love. I love You. Amen.

I am treasured

"For we are God's masterpiece." Ephesians 2:10 (NLT)

When I was born, my mom bought me a white teddy bear with a red bow the same size as me. Every month for a year, she took a picture of me next to it. As I grew, I loved that bear. When I was a toddler, I couldn't sleep unless the bear was beside me. I hate to admit it, but even in elementary school, I remember holding on to that bear after having a bad day. I treasured it so much. My mom had a challenging time even washing it because I wouldn't let it out of my sight.

Jesus treasures us in the same way, but loves us so much more! One of the many encouragements Jesus taught His disciples was how much God treasured them. Luke tells us that when Jesus was about to send out His twelve best friends to do some preaching and teaching for Him, He reminded them before they left: "Not one [sparrow] will fall to the ground outside your Father's care. And even the very hairs of your head are all numbered. So don't be afraid; you are worth more than many sparrows" (Matthew 10:29-31, NIV).

Jesus was telling them God loved them more than they could ever imagine or fathom.

"Long before he laid down earth's foundations, he had us in mind, had settled on us as the focus of his love, to be made whole and holy by his love. Long, long ago he decided to adopt us into his family through Jesus Christ. (What pleasure he took in planning this!) He wanted us to enter into the celebration of his lavish gift-giving by the hand of his beloved Son." Ephesians 1:4-6 (MSG)

The same is true of us today. Just as He has loved you from the beginning of time, He has treasured you, too. You are His workmanship, His masterpiece. He knows the number of hairs on your head. He knows your every strength and weakness yet calls you His best creation.

Challenge: There's a practice called imagination meditation[1] that Christians use to draw closer to God. Close your eyes and imagine Jesus hugging you. Imagine Him telling you how special and treasured you are to Him. Sit a while and feel His presence. Tell Him anything you want to say and listen to His response.

Prayer: Thank You, Jesus, for the reminder that I am your precious treasure. I know You love me and are working on my behalf. Thank You for loving me and creating me this way. Remind me of these truths today. I love You. Amen.

I am adored

"The Lord your God is with you [and His Name is Jesus], the Mighty Warrior who saves. He will take great delight in you"
Zephaniah 3:17a (NIV)

A little fun fact about me—I am a massive fan of those sappy love stories. Give me a rom-com, and I'll soak it up. Who doesn't want to step into a world where the guy and girl always fall in love and where the problems are always fixed with a happily-ever-after?

Growing up, I loved to imagine myself as the girl who the prince would come and rescue. I realized in my teen years, however, that I already had a Prince who had saved me and absolutely adored me. Not in some sappy, romantic way, but in a real, sacrificial love way that's never failing and never-ending. And guess what? He's saved you too and looks at you adoringly too.

"I have loved you with an everlasting love; therefore I have continued my faithfulness to you." Jeremiah 31:3

Maybe you're in a place where it seems like no one sees, no one cares. Don't lose hope, friend. Jesus sees, and He cares. He's your Knight in shining armor who came to save you from death and sin. He rejoices over you. He takes delight in what you do, what you say, and who you are. He adores you.

Challenge: Do you believe you are loved by King Jesus? Take a moment to sit quietly. No phone, no music, just silence. Let Jesus' presence fill your mind. He's with you now. Breathe in His love and care, and breathe out any doubt. Just be with Him. He will meet you where you are.

Prayer: You adore me, Jesus. Thank You for seeing me and for knowing me. Help me believe this truth today. Help me to live a life that demonstrates to others that You love me. I love You. Amen.

I am remembered

"He will be with you; He will not leave you or forsake you. Do not fear or be dismayed." Deuteronomy 31:8

A few years ago, my family and friends forgot my birthday. Has that ever happened to you? I hope it never does. It stinks. I felt so lonely and hurt and then I got angry. How dare they forget my birthday? But really, I was just sad. Didn't I matter to them?

God taught me through that experience that sometimes people will disappoint us, even people very close to us. Sometimes, the people around us will forget us. But God will never forget us. He remembered me on my birthday, and He celebrated me. I felt even closer to Him because of the whole ordeal.

God promises us that He'll never leave us or forsake us. To forsake means to abandon or leave. So, God promises never to leave us and always to remember us.

"And we know for those who love God all things work together for good, for those who are called according to His purpose."
Romans 8:28

I know sometimes it seems as if God has forgotten about us. It's tempting to believe He's overlooked us when terrible things happen and our world no longer makes sense. But hold on to this promise: God loves you and is working on your behalf. He remembers you, so don't worry. Choose to trust Him, even in those hard times.

Challenge: Memorize Romans 8:28. It's gotten me through some hard days. Meditate on this verse and spend time praying for His intervention on your behalf.

Prayer: Jesus, thank You for promising never to leave me or forget about me. Thank You for always taking care of me. Thank You for Your love for me. I love You. Amen.

Journal

Part II

I am created

"My frame was not hidden from You, when I was being made in secret, intricately woven in the depths of the earth."

Psalm 139:15

I am created

"Then God said, 'Let us make man in our likeness.'"
Genesis 1:26

The very first thing God did was create. "In the beginning, God created" (Genesis 1:1). He started with light and continued with forming the earth, waters, land, and animals. The climax, however, was yet to come. On the sixth day, God created humans.

God spoke to no other creation as He did to Adam, the first man. One whole chapter describes the creation of man and woman (Genesis 2). That's not a coincidence. Everything God does has a purpose. Like creating you - that was not a mistake either.

"But now, O Lord, you are our Father; we are the clay, and you are our potter; we are all the work of your hand." Isaiah 64:8

As God is the Potter, we are His clay. The psalmist David wrote, "You knitted me together in my mother's womb. I praise you, for I am fearfully and wonderfully made" (Psalm 139:13-14). God saw you in your mother's womb. You were on God's mind even before your parents thought to have you. You're not an accident. You're created to fulfill a purpose. You were chosen at birth. You are God's masterpiece He carefully and creatively molded and formed with His wisdom and understanding.

Nothing God creates is a mistake or an accident - It's impossible for the God of the universe, who knows the beginning from the end, to make a mistake. It's not in His nature. So don't believe the lie that you're not worth it, unique, or loved. You were specially created for such a time as this: with this family, this ethnicity, in this nation, in this year, for this school or workplace, with these classmates or these coworkers, and this life. You are created by a Master Designer who has never and will never make a mistake.

Challenge: Take a walk outside today and count the beautiful things you see around you. Write a list in your mind and add yourself to your list. Spend time thanking God for all the beauty you see around you.

Prayer: Thank You, God, for creating me! Thank You for life and breath each day I'm alive. Thank You for the way You have made me. Help me see myself through Your eyes today. I love You. Amen

I am the image of God

"So God created man in His own image, in the image of God He created him; male and female He created them."
Genesis 1:27

While I taught middle school, one of my favorite spirit wear days was when teachers and students dressed as each other for the day. Teachers tried to match the teenager fashion at the time, while students chose a teacher to dress like. Most students dressed as the P.E. teacher because who doesn't want to wear sweatpants and a t-shirt to school? But I loved it when my students would dress up like me – I felt seen and acknowledged when they took the time to choose what outfit Mrs. Djokoto would wear.

More than just dressing up like God, we were created *like* God, we were made in the same image of Him. We have heard that often, but do we know what that means? Think about it this way. Who is God? What attributes does God have? He is good, holy, righteous, pure, loving, and beautiful. Those same attributes describe you, too, since you're made in His image. Another Bible version says in His likeness. You are like God - a mirror image. You are good, holy, righteous, pure, loving, and beautiful. And so much more.

"When God created man, He made him in the likeness of God."
Genesis 5:1

That does not mean we always act like God. Paul writes in Colossians that we are to dress like or "put on" the traits of compassion, kindness, humility, and patience (Colossians 3:12). Because of the sin in our lives, we often act just the opposite way. That's not how God created us to be, however. Our DNA is programmed to be like God. Through the power of the Holy Spirit, it is our choice to reflect His image or not.

Challenge: Stand in front of the mirror and tell yourself you are beautiful (and mean it). Read Genesis 1:27 aloud and imagine yourself in the Garden of Eden, the first woman God created. You are just as beautiful to God as the first sinless Eve was. You were created in His image!

Prayer: Thank You, Lord, for creating me in Your image. You are good and holy, righteous and pure. Please help me make choices today that reflect Your goodness to the world around me. I love you. Amen.

I am a masterpiece

"My frame was not hidden from You, when I was being made in secret, intricately woven in the depths of the earth."
Psalm 139:15

I am not all that into science, but have you ever thought about how you were formed intricately in your mother's womb? You might now be thinking *Yuck!* But it's interesting to think about. Doctors say a baby is the size of a pea for the first month and grows into the size of a bean by the second[2]. During that time, your brain, spine, arms, and legs form. Can you imagine? A pea with arms and legs and a brain? It is a funny picture. But then you think about how different each of us is and how God has formed you in the womb. Your color, your shape, your genes, your DNA, your personality - All are created during then as well. God has intricately made every part of you.

"You are God's masterpiece." Ephesians 2:10 (NLT)

That means that all of you - your strengths, your weaknesses, your likes, your dislikes, your personality, your hair color, your height, your metabolism – everything is part of God's masterpiece, which is you. Next time you start hating something about yourself, stop and think about this fact: God created you that way. That should give us way better self-confidence because God does not make mistakes.

Growing up, I always hated my height. I was always the tallest girl in the class, taller than all the boys, too, which was not cool in my mind. During presentations, I was always a head taller than all the other pupils. I hated being tall. I felt awkward and weird. But I learned through the years that God did not make a mistake in making me extra tall. He knew exactly what He was doing when He put height in my DNA. I've come to appreciate my height now. Thankfully, I met a man taller than me, my now husband. I am thankful for being tall because I can often turn that extra height into confidence that I lack in certain circumstances. So don't discount the things about yourself that you don't like right now. Be patient; one day, I think you will see why God made you that way.

Challenge: Make a list of your strengths and weaknesses and thank God for each one. Yes, even your shortcomings, because He made you that way for a reason. Try to list more strengths than weaknesses. Reflect on the fact that you are God's extraordinary masterpiece.

Prayer: Lord, thank You for taking the time to create me in my mother's womb intricately. Thank You for the gift of life. Thank You for calling me Your masterpiece. Help me believe it. I love You. Amen.

I am beautiful

"He has made everything beautiful in its time."
Ecclesiastes 3:11

All of us want to be beautiful. Our society defines beauty in a very different way than what God outlines in Scripture. Magazines, billboards, commercials, social media – all telling us we need to be skinnier, curvier, lighter, or darker. It is easy to subconsciously start to compare ourselves with those models who define beauty to the world around us.

But that's not what God says is beautiful. "For the Lord sees not as man sees: Man looks on the outward appearance, but the Lord looks on the heart" (1 Samuel 16:7). God is more focused on what our hearts look like. He defines beauty as "a woman who fears the Lord" (Proverbs 31:30).

"Charm is deceitful, and beauty is vain, but a woman who fears the Lord is to be praised." Proverbs 31:30

Remember also that God created you as His masterpiece. Therefore, of course, He finds you beautiful, just the way you are. You don't need to change a thing to please God. You are His most beautiful masterpiece. It's sometimes hard to remember this truth when we're constantly comparing ourselves to others. What we repeat to ourselves in our minds matters, so what we believe about ourselves should be grounded in the Word of God.

Challenge: Today, instead of going on social media and comparing yourself with others, take that time to read your Bible. Whatever you put into your mind will eventually come out, so try filling it with truth. If you are new to Bible reading, try reading the book of Psalms, like Psalm 139. It is a beautiful book of poems that reflect our hearts and souls.

Prayer: Lord, help me remember that beauty is not defined by what others tell me. Help me believe I am beautiful to You. Silence the lies that the world tells me. Thank You for creating me this way. I love You. Amen.

I am uniquely me

"By the word of the LORD the heavens were made, and by the breath of His mouth all their host. Let all the earth fear the LORD; let all the inhabitants of the world stand in awe of Him! For He spoke, and it came to be; He commanded, and it stood firm." Psalm 33:3, 5-6

Have you heard that no two snowflakes are the same? Every single snowflake that falls to the ground has a unique design. According to a mathematician named Ethan Siegal, approximately 10^{34} snowflakes have fallen in the history of our world[3]. That's billions and billions and billions of snowflakes. And they are all unique? That's what the scientists have found. That's how creative God is!

The same goes for people. How many different people groups and languages and skin tones and personalities are there? Researchers say there are over seven thousand languages[4], six hundred fifty ethnicities[5], and one hundred skin tones[6] in our world, with more being discovered daily. So many different combinations are possible! You are totally unique. You are you for a reason, too.

"I praise You for I am fearfully and wonderfully made. Wonderful are Your works; my soul knows it very well." Psalm 139:14

God made you uniquely YOU for a reason. It is not by accident. He formed you in your mother's womb perfectly. Wonderfully. He created you with your height, weight, eye color, hair color, personality, gifts, and talents. You are no mistake. You are His incredible masterpiece and His beautiful creation.

Challenge: Draw a web around your name and try to list everything that makes you *you* – Your personality, your family background, your ethnicity, etc. Spend time in prayer, thanking God for making you this way.

Prayer: Wow, God! You created everything so uniquely! Thank You for the ways You show Your creativity to me every day: the beautiful sunset, the snowflakes in the sky,

Journal

Journal

Part III

I am saved

"Because, if you confess with your mouth that Jesus is Lord and believe in your heart that God raised him from the dead, you will be saved."

Romans 10:9

I am saved

"Because, if you confess with your mouth that Jesus is Lord and believe in your heart that God raised him from the dead, you will be saved." Romans 10:9

We deserve to die. That's the most blunt way I can say it. I deserve death and separation from God forever. I am a sinner. I have sinned against God and others too many times to count. Yes, overall, I may be a good person, not too bad, but even that one sin committed deserves punishment. And according to the law, that punishment is death.

"For the wages of sin is death" Romans 6:23

In the beginning, after God created Adam and Eve, He gave them authority over all creation to eat and feast on whatever their hearts desired. But there was one tree He knew that if they ate from it, their eyes would be opened to good and evil. They would know shame, guilt, fear, and sin. We know the rest of the story. They ate, sin entered, and their punishment was banishment. Sin cannot be in the presence of a holy God.

Adam and Eve deserved death once they disobeyed God. But in His mercy, God let them live. And not only live but continue having a relationship with God. Though harder and somewhat stained with sin in the picture, God didn't banish them entirely from His presence.

"For the wages of sin is death, but the free gift of God is eternal life in Christ Jesus our Lord." Romans 6:23 (emphasis added)

I like how it says it is a free gift. Though we deserve to die and be separated from God, He chose a different way. He died in our place so we could live with God forever instead. Read that sentence again. Jesus died in our place and on our behalf so that you and I could be saved. Forever. Wow. Now that is something to celebrate.

Challenge: Have you ever surrendered your life to Jesus? Or have you been going along with the motions, never committing fully? I challenge you to think about what you believe. Do you believe Jesus died for you so you could have a relationship with Him? Have you surrendered to Him fully? Take time to pray and listen to what God is telling you.

Prayer: Jesus, thank You for dying on my behalf. Thank You for giving me eternal and abundant life for free. Thank You for saving me, especially when I could never earn it. Jesus, I believe in You and that You did all these things for me. I confess I have not lived a life entirely devoted to you. Please help me follow You. I give You my life. I love You. Amen.

**Note: If you prayed this prayer for the first time, welcome to the family, sister! I would encourage you to tell someone you trust. Find a good church, read the Bible, and grow in your faith. It is a process, so don't be too hard on yourself. Jesus will guide you through the process; you won't go alone. He is now living with you and will never forsake you. You are His, and He is yours.

I am forgiven

"For this is my blood of the covenant, which is poured out for many for the forgiveness of sins." Matthew 26:28

Have you ever done something that you think God cannot forgive? I have. I have found myself weeping over things I have done, knowing I deserve whatever punishment, but also pleading for God to forgive me and make things right.

The amazing thing is that He always does. Even when I mess up repeatedly, He is faithful to forgive me each time.

"He does not deal with us according to our sins, nor repay us according to our iniquities. For as high as the heavens are above the earth, so great is His steadfast love toward those who fear Him; as far as the east is from the west, so far does He remove our transgressions from us." Psalm 103:10-12

He does the same for you. As high as the heavens are above the earth, so great is His love for you. As far as the east is from the west, so far does He remove our sins from us. He does not remember our sins or hold them against us. He forgives us. No matter what. That is the kind of God He is.

Ashley Djokoto

So next time you are wallowing in guilt, pleading for God to forgive you, remember this verse and speak it over yourself. You are loved. You are saved. You are forgiven.

Challenge: We do have a role to play in our forgiveness. It is called confession. God makes it clear that we need to humble ourselves and ask Him for forgiveness for our sins. Make a goal once a day to confess your sins to God. Make it a habit. The more you do it, the more you will realize you need His forgiveness. This is a good thing. We all sin, but it takes humility to admit it and ask for forgiveness.

Prayer: Thank You, Jesus, for always forgiving me. Thank You for the cross and for saving me from sin and death. Thank You for your steadfast love that will never fail me. I love You, Lord. Amen.

I am redeemed

"Fear not, for I have redeemed you; I have called you by name; you are mine." Isaiah 43:1

To redeem means to clear someone from a debt. We had a vast, insurmountable debt with God. One that Christ removed on our behalf at no cost to us. It is like a banker who forgives a man his loan without any repercussions for the man. Not only does he forgive his debt, but he pays for it out of his own pocket. That is what Christ has done for us. He has taken our debt, our sin, and put it on His own shoulders.

"Christ redeemed us from the curse of the law by becoming a curse for us." Galatians 3:13

When Jesus was on the cross, He took all of our sins with him: all our lies and half-truths, disrespectful attitudes and thoughts, shame and regrets, jealousy and discontentment, and impure thoughts and actions. Every sin you have ever committed and will commit was nailed to the cross on that dark day.

But the story does not end there. On the third day, He defeated death and rose again to new life. Through His blood, he banished all our sins and made a way to redeem us.

"Indeed, under the law, almost everything is purified with blood, and without the shedding of blood, there is no forgiveness of sins."
Hebrews 9:22

    Without His blood, there would be no redemption. And so, He had to die in our place to make a way for us to have this relationship with God. Isn't that amazing?! God wanted a relationship with us so much that He gave His Son as a sacrifice for us. To die in our place so we can be with Him forever. That is God's amazing plan of redemption.

Challenge: Read Hebrews 9:11-28. Meditate on the truths found in this passage. How does God show His love for us? Why did Christ die for us? What do we get out of His once-for-all sacrifice?

Prayer: Thank You, God, for sending Your Son to redeem me. I know I am a sinner and don't deserve Your forgiveness. But because of Jesus' work on the cross, I know I am forgiven and redeemed. Thank you! I love You. Amen.

I am restored

"When Adam sinned, sin entered the world. Adam's sin brought death, so death spread to everyone, for everyone sinned… For the sin of this one man, Adam, brought death to many. But even greater is God's wonderful grace and his gift of forgiveness to many through this other man, Jesus Christ… Yes, Adam's one sin brings condemnation for everyone, but Christ's one act of righteousness brings a right relationship with God and new life for everyone. Because one person disobeyed God, many became sinners. But because one other person obeyed God, many will be made righteous." Romans 5:12, 15, 18-19 (NLT)

God's desire was for people to live in harmony with Him forever in the Garden of Eden, a land flowing with milk and honey. But because of one man's choice, we were all banished from that paradise. It does not quite seem fair, does it? Yet, God made a way for us to be restored to that place where we are with God forever, through one man: Jesus Christ. If we believe in Him and give our lives to Him, He promises to restore us to that place of shalom (peace). It is God's great story of redemption and restoration.

I love watching videos where people take a rough, beaten-up, ugly piece of furniture and make it chic, beautiful, and clean. I love seeing the transformation. It looks easy, but I know it must be a difficult and expensive project. Things must go wrong in the process, but the transformation happens, nonetheless. That is what God does with us. We come to Him dirty with all our sins and failures, and He restores us, making us clean, whole, and beautiful. Just like the furniture, though, it does not come without bumps and bruises on the way. We have to give up certain sins and pleasures that are not holy. We have to go through God's molding and remolding process of sanctification, but ultimately, we are transformed completely.

"And after you have suffered a little while, the God of all grace, who has called you to His eternal glory in Christ, will Himself restore, confirm, strengthen, and establish you." 1 Peter 5:10

Though the process of this sanctification isn't always pleasant at the time, we can be assured that He is restoring us to glory in Christ. And slowly but surely, we will become more like our Savior who will one day bring our restoration to a completion when He comes again (Acts 3:21).

Challenge: Draw a picture of the "old" you and list all your old habits. Tear it up and throw it in the garbage because God has made you new!

Prayer: Thank You, Lord, for restoring me, for never giving up on me. Thank You for Your plan of redemption and restoration for our world. Thank you for letting me be a part of it. Thank You for not leaving me as I am but restoring me to who You've created me to be. I love You. Amen.

I am a new creation

"Therefore, if anyone is in Christ, [she] is a new creation. The old has passed away; behold, the new has come."
2 Corinthians 5:17

If we accept Jesus as our Savior and follow Him with our lives, He makes us brand new. Isn't that an amazing promise?!

When I was born, my parents gave me a special blanket. I slept with that thing every night for the first five years of my life. By age six, I had worn it down to tatters and holes. My mom and I decided to try to wash it and see if we could make it clean again. (It was starting to smell.) Unfortunately, it didn't come out clean; it came out more torn. I cried because all I had left of my blanket was one small corner. Sometimes, we try to make things clean on our own but make a mess of it instead. Thankfully, God has no problem making us pure, whole, and brand new.

One day, we will all stand before His great throne in heaven. What will He say to you when you stand before Him? If you have committed your life to Him, I have complete confidence that He'll look at you and see no blemishes, stains, or sins. He will see Jesus' blood covering you and making you look as white as snow.

"Though your sins are like scarlet, I will make them as white as snow. Though they are red like crimson, I will make them like wool." Isaiah 1:18

He will see you as His child, beautiful, forgiven, and new. So, friend, there is no need to hold on to that shame, guilt, or fear. Let it go and trust the promises He has given us. You are completely forgiven. You are beautiful in His sight. You are a new creation.

Challenge: There is this really cool science experiment that shows us what it looks like for God to forgive us. If you put water in a clear jar and add lots of food coloring, it will turn into darker-colored water. That is like our hearts when there's sin in us. But then, if you pour just one drop of bleach water into the mixture, it turns back into clear water. It is pretty amazing to watch. That is like what God does to our hearts when He forgives us. Look up the "Jesus, Sin & You" video on YouTube to see it for yourself.

Prayer: Thank You, Jesus, for Your sacrifice that purifies me and gives me new life. Thank You for forgiving me. Thank you for Your steadfast love and mercies that are new every day. Help me follow You. I love You. Amen.

Journal

Part IV

I am made righteous

"For our sake He made Him to be sin who knew no sin, so that in Him we might become the righteousness of God."

2 Corinthians 5:21

I am made righteous

"For our sake He made Him to be sin who knew no sin, so that in Him we might become the righteousness of God."
2 Corinthians 5:21

Righteousness is simply living rightly or having a right relationship with God and others. In the Bible, God often tells us there is great reward in living righteously. Throughout the books of Psalms and Proverbs, the authors compare the righteous person to the wicked person and the kinds of endings they are sure to have.

"Blessed are they who observe justice, who do righteousness at all times!" Psalm 106:3

But as we see countless times before in the lives of people like King David, who chose adultery; Abraham, who lied; Noah, who got drunk; Peter, who denied Christ; and Rahab, who seduced men – men and women God used significantly in the Bible – it is impossible to live a completely righteous life. We all mess up. We all are prone to sin, even if we are saved. We can never do enough good things to get right with God. Never.

But that is good news. Because God knew that we could never do enough good things to get right with Him, He sent His Son to become our righteousness for us. When we stand before Him one day, God will not see us but Christ, the only perfectly righteous person who has ever lived. Jesus took on the world's sins to make us righteous before God. Amazing.

> *"More than that, we also rejoice in God through our Lord Jesus Christ, through whom we have now received reconciliation."*
> *Romans 5:11*

Challenge: List the "good" things you've done this week. Now, rip them up and throw them away. Our good deeds are like filthy rags compared to Jesus (Romans 3:8). Thankfully, Jesus does not need our good deeds; He gave us Himself to be our righteousness. Spend time thanking Him for His sacrifice.

Prayer: Thank You, Jesus, for the cross. Thank You for taking my sins so that I can be considered righteous before God. Thank You for living a perfect life on earth and making this possible. I love You. Amen.

I am justified

"He saved us, not because of works done by us in righteousness, but according to his own mercy ... so that being justified by his grace we might become heirs according to the hope of eternal life."
Titus 3:5, 7

We can never be good enough to get to heaven or to get right with God. However, the world likes to tell us the opposite: "I'm not that bad of a person, so I don't have to worry about going to hell." Have you heard that before? Or have you thought it? Maybe you've thought, how can a good God put good people in hell?

Let me ask you this: what is good? Everyone's definition of good is different. One person thinks lying is not that bad or disobeying parents isn't a big deal, yet God's Word tells us to avoid such things (2 Timothy 3:2-5). If we use our definition of good, we are missing the point. It is God who created us and the world. Don't you think He deserves to set the bar for what is good and evil?

God is perfect, holy, and pure. No sin can even come close to Him. When sinful, unclean people tried in the Old Testament, without going through the proper cleansing rituals that God had ordained, they died on the spot (Leviticus 10:1-2). That is how holy God is. It is within reason, then, that we need to be just as holy to reach God.

How, then, are we justified? How can we reach God, if not by being better? How could we ever hope to be in a right relationship with our Father?

"Therefore, since we have been justified through faith, we have peace with God through our Lord Jesus Christ" Romans 5:1

The amazing truth is that God freely gives us the gift of justification through His Son's death and resurrection. When we accept Jesus as our Lord and Savior, we are completely justified. There is nothing *we* could ever think, do, or say that could bring us into a right relationship with God. It's only by grace we are saved (Ephesians 2:5). Only through believing His Son died in our place so that we can have a relationship with Himself can this justification occur.

Challenge: Read all of Romans 5. Take note of what God does for us and what we could never in a million years do. Spend time thanking God for this beautiful gift.

Prayer: Thank You, God, for making a way for me to be justified, or to be made right with You. Thank You that I cannot do it on my own, lest my pride get in the way. Help me remember it is not about doing good works to get in Your good graces; instead, it is a free gift from You. I love You. Amen.

I am delivered

"He has delivered us from the domain of darkness and transferred up to the kingdom of His beloved Son, in whom we have redemption, the forgiveness of sins."
Colossians 1:13-14

I love those stories where the prince rides in and saves the damsel in distress, and they live happily ever after. There are so many books and movies out there with that theme. Nowadays, the female is the hero more often than not, but the idea is still the same – deliverance from the foes. The hero saves the world from complete annihilation. The team of good guys beats the bad guys. The universe is saved from the end of the world. You get the point.

We all need deliverance, don't we? Maybe it is not from the world's end, but we all need saving from something or someone. From bad grades, a breakup, anxiety, depression, addiction, the list goes on. In reality, most of the time, we need someone to help us because we tend to mess things up over and over again.

The beautiful, incredible thing is that we cannot deliver ourselves from what we most need deliverance from - spiritual death because of the sin and brokenness in us. You might be thinking – wait, why is that beautiful and amazing? That sounds like a disaster. It would be if it were not for God's plan.

"But God shows His love for us in that while we were still sinners, Christ died for us." Romans 5:8

God's plan for us started before the foundation of the world. He chose His Son, Jesus, to live among humans as a human to show His extreme love for us. He took it a step further and asked His Son to die the most terrible death – physically and spiritually – so that we may be delivered from ours. We are delivered because Christ died and took all our sins upon Himself. We are completely and fully delivered. Now, we have life. We have love, hope, forgiveness, and every spiritual blessing in Christ. The list goes on and on. That is the beauty of God's plan. That is the wonder of it. How could God love us so much to deliver us from the death we deserved?

"Blessed be the God and Father of our Lord Jesus Christ, who has blessed us in Christ with every spiritual blessing in the heavenly places, even as He chose us in Him before the foundation of the world, that we should be holy and blameless before Him." Ephesians 1:3-4

Challenge: Read Ephesians 1 and list our spiritual blessings in Jesus. Spend time thanking God for His deliverance out of spiritual death and into life.

Prayer: Thank You, Father, for Your deep and compassionate love for me. Thank You for delivering me from sin and death. Forgive me for the ways I have wronged You in the past. Thank You for every spiritual blessing I have in You. I love You. Amen.

I am faith-filled

"Though you have not seen Him, you love Him. Though you do not now see Him, you believe in Him and rejoice with joy that is inexpressible and filled with glory, obtaining the outcome of your faith – the salvation of your souls"
1 Peter 1:8-9

Have you ever seen a Middle Eastern tapestry? They are beautiful. All the intricate designs woven together flawlessly. It is truly amazing to look at and think about how it was made. We can think of our faith journeys as those tapestries. God weaves together our stories in unique and intricate ways. We cannot even fathom what He's going to do in our lives from beginning to end (Ecclesiastes 3:11).

Could I have imagined where God would lead me when I was growing up? Could I have known how God would grow me and transform me from a shy teenager into the leader I am today? Could I have foreseen the amazing things I have had the opportunity to do and the diverse people I have gotten to meet through this life? The answer is no to all of the above. God has an amazing story for each one of us – and each is different and unique. And through each event and encounter, God is growing our faith in Him more and more. For example, when I moved to Ghana, I was terrified of leaving all my friends and family behind. I had my first panic attack when I signed the contract and bought the tickets. But through my time here, I have grown so much in my faith. I am not the same woman I was when I left America those nine years ago.

As I have grown up more and more in my faith, I can see that it is not me who's getting better at having faith; it is the Holy Spirit who gives me more faith. More faith to face whatever challenges are in front of me, more faith to pray though the circumstances seem hopeless, and more faith to keep walking with Him. And it is Jesus alone who will one day lead me Home with the faith He has given me. How amazing is that? Here is a promise to leave you with today:

"May the God of hope fill you with all joy and peace in believing, so that by the power of the Holy Spirit you may abound in hope."
Romans 15:13

May you abound in joy, peace, and more faith today, friend. May your life be filled with more of Jesus. May you experience His presence like never before. And may He take center stage in your heart.

Challenge: Write down or tell someone your faith story. How did you meet Jesus? How has He changed your life? How has He filled you with more faith?

Prayer: Thank You for Your saving faith, Lord. Thank You that it ALL comes from You, and I can never mess it up too much. Thank You for this journey You have placed me on. Please give me more faith as I trust You more every day. I love You. Amen.

I am clothed in righteousness

"I will greatly rejoice in the Lord; my soul shall exult in my God, for He has clothed me with the garments of salvation; He has covered me with the robe of righteousness... as a bride adorns herself with her jewels." Isaiah 61:10

Read that verse again. Who is it that clothes us in salvation and righteousness? It is God, not us. I love this verse. I can picture a bride walking down the aisle to her groom, adorned in precious jewelry, with flowers in her hair and a train of white following her every step. Sigh. Who doesn't love a good wedding? God compares this lovely bride to one who is clothed in righteousness and salvation. It is a beautiful thing to be clothed in righteousness.

If you are a Christian, a Jesus follower, this promise is for you. You are that beautiful bride, clothed in righteousness in God's eyes. He doesn't see that lie you told last week, that sarcastic comment you made to your mom, or even that gossip you started. He sees His garment of righteousness on your shoulders, and He is ready to meet you at the end of the aisle.

"And now the prize awaits me—the crown of righteousness, which the Lord, the righteous Judge, will give me on the day of His return. And the prize is not just for me but for all who eagerly look forward to His appearing." 2 Timothy 4:8 (NLT)

Now, that does not excuse us from giving in to our sins and struggles. God has given us His Spirit, the Holy Spirit, to help us fight against our fleshly desires and live according to His Word (Romans 8:1-11). God expects us to obey Him as any child would abide by their loving father. But when we mess up, because we will, He will forgive us and not let the robe of righteousness slip from our shoulders. He will remove those sins as far as the east is from the west (Psalm 103:12). We will be welcomed into the King's kingdom, clothed in the beautiful garments of salvation and righteousness, as a bride coming home to her Beloved. Now, that is a beautiful promise.

Challenge: Read Romans 8:1-11. Now, read it again. Highlight every time it says "Spirit" and "life." Notice what Christ's role in bringing us life is. Notice what comes in the way of that life.

Prayer: Lord Jesus, I thank You for clothing me in righteousness. Especially because I don't deserve it. Thank You for always forgiving me and helping me with my sin struggle. Thank You for putting the Holy Spirit in me, who guides me and corrects me. Please help me live a righteous life in obedience. I love You. Amen.

Journal

Part V

I am being made like Christ

"For it is God who works in you, both to will and to act for His good pleasure."

Philippians 2:13

I am being made like Christ

"Beloved, we are God's children now, and what we will be has not yet appeared; but we know that when He appears we shall be like Him, because we shall see Him as he is."
1 John 3:2

It is a process: this thing called sanctification – the process of being made like Jesus. It will not happen the second you're saved. It will take a lifetime of hard work and discipline. It will not always be easy. You will have to make sacrifices, and you will have to surrender. You will need to learn to humble yourself when you know you're right and forgive when they don't deserve it. You will need to put others first, even when tired and anxious. It is not an easy road, this Christian walk. But every step you take will be worth it.

"Join with me in suffering, like a good soldier of Christ Jesus. No one serving as a soldier gets entangled in civilian affairs, but rather tries to please his commanding officer. Similarly, anyone who competes as an athlete does not receive the victor's crown except by competing according to the rules. The hardworking farmer should be the first to receive a share of the crops."
2 Timothy 2:3-6 (NIV)

Paul is writing to his good friend, Timothy, reminding him that in the world, we will have trouble, but Christ has overcome all of that for us (John 16:33). As Jesus' followers, we, then, need to be separated from the world like officers in the army. We need to exhibit discipline like athletes training for the Olympics and be hardworking like farmers, striving to feed their families. Some Christians live like God tells us to kick back and relax because we're saved, and nothing can harm us. But that is nowhere in Scripture. The opposite is: we need to train ourselves now, learn to be disciplined, and finish our race strong (1 Corinthians 9:24). But take heart, friends! It is not you who sanctifies you. It is God Himself who shares in this burden –He takes the burden off of us and onto Himself.

"For it is God who works in you, both to will and to act for His good pleasure." Philippians 2:13

God is the One who molds us and slowly forms us into a new creation. He is the One who convicts, loves, and shows us kindness that leads us to repentance (Romans 2:4). He will not forsake you in this. Trust that He is working in you, even today. Will you listen? Will you obey?

Challenge: Look up verses about the spiritual disciplines. What habits or disciplines can you start practicing more of in your life? Make a commitment and pray, asking God to help you do these things more.

Prayer: Lord, thank You for Your never-failing faithfulness and for saving me so I may have this amazing relationship with You. Forgive me for all the ways I have messed up. Please help me learn to discipline myself so I can look more like You. Help me to imitate You in everything I do and say today. I love You. Amen.

I am Spirit-led

"For I know that good itself does not dwell in me, that is, in my sinful nature. For I have the desire to do what is good, but I cannot carry it out. For I do not do the good I want to do, but the evil I do not want to do—this I keep on doing… So I find this law at work: Although I want to do good, evil is right there with me. For in my inner being I delight in God's law; but I see another law at work in me, waging war against the law of my mind and making me a prisoner of the law of sin at work within me." Romans 7:18-19, 21-23

There is an old cartoon where a man is trying to make a decision, and he has an angel on one shoulder and the devil on the other. The angel whispers in his ear to do the right thing, while the devil whispers the wrong choice. We may not have an angel or the devil sitting on our shoulders, but we do have the same kind of internal war inside us every day. Will we obey our sinful flesh, or will we follow the Holy Spirit in us?

Let me put it this way: Have you ever known you shouldn't do something, but you did it anyway? "Oh, I know I should study, but this show is just too good – I'll watch one more episode." "I know I should get up early to read my Bible, but I was up late, and I'm tired." "I probably shouldn't be alone with my boyfriend tonight, but nothing will happen." We have all been there. We have all made choices we knew weren't good for us, but we did it anyway. Those are moments when we let our flesh lead us.

"Those who live according to the flesh have their minds set on what the flesh desires; but those who live in accordance with the Spirit have their minds set on what the Spirit desires. The mind governed by the flesh is death, but the mind governed by the Spirit is life and peace… For if you live according to the flesh, you will die; but if by the Spirit you put to death the deeds of the body, you will live. For those who are led by the Spirit of God are the [daughters] of God." Romans 8: 5-6, 13-14

I love this passage. All hope is not lost! Though we are sinful, and we often mess up, there is hope. God has made a way through the Holy Spirit – His Spirit living in us – that we can put to death the deeds of the flesh so we can live. We can choose to live according to God's Spirit in us. I know it is not easy, but God will enable us to walk in the Spirit, to live according to the Spirit. All we need to do is surrender. When we mess up, because we will, we can repent and start over. Slowly but surely, we will learn how to say no to our flesh and live by the Spirit a little more each day.

Challenge: Make a list of ways you have lived by the flesh versus lived by the Spirit in the last week. Be honest with yourself. Confess those sins to God and commit to follow Him today. Pray and ask Him to help you say no to your flesh and follow Him.

Prayer: Thank You, Lord, for life! Thank You for putting Your Spirit inside us, the same Spirit that rose Jesus from the dead is in me – How amazing! I confess that I've been living according to my flesh; please forgive me. Please help me put to death my sinful nature and choose to follow You today. I love You. Amen.

I am dead to self

"I have been crucified with Christ. It is no longer I who live, but Christ who lives in me. And the life I now live in the flesh I live by faith in the Son of God, who loved me and gave himself for me." Galatians 2:20

No one wants to die. Not really. God has made us to have the will to survive inside of us. We yearn to be alive and truly live. That is why so many people are chasing things they think can give them true life: more money, more sex, more power, more friends, more fame. But those things cannot bring life the way Jesus can. Only Jesus can give us the abundant life we yearn for (John 10:10). He did it by dying on the cross. But not even Jesus wanted to die. Luke 22:44 tells us that Jesus was so agonized over dying on the cross He sweat blood. Scientists now know that it was a case of Hematidrosis, a condition caused by great fear or stress that causes a person's sweat to turn into drops of blood[7].

Yet, though He did not want to die, and though He was either so stressed or so afraid (or both), He sweat drops of blood, He did it anyways - for you. He told His Father, "Not my will, but Yours be done" (Luke 22:42). And that is the same thing He asks of His followers today.

"For whoever would save his life will lose it, but whoever loses his life for My sake and the gospel's will save it." Mark 8:35

To have the abundant life Jesus died to give us, we must be willing to give up our lives for Him. We must die to ourselves. We must take up our cross and follow Him (Matthew 10:38). Maybe that means not watching a particular show or listening to music that profanes His Name. Maybe that means forgiving someone who hurt you deeply. Perhaps it means giving up your possessions and moving across the world to be a missionary. Maybe it means talking to your friends about what Jesus has done for you. None of these are easy things to do. They will require us to lay down our desires and choose to follow Jesus no matter what. Some may laugh at us, others may mock, and some may disown you, but be encouraged, sister, your heavenly Father sees you and knows you and has made a home for you with Him forever.

Challenge: Pray and ask God how you can serve Him today. What is one thing you can do that would require giving up something for His kingdom? Commit to doing that one thing today.

Prayer: Lord Jesus, thank You for dying for me, though it caused You great stress. Thank You for giving up Your life so I could have abundant life. Please help me die to myself today. Show me someone I could serve or something I could give up today. Show me how I can die to myself and choose the abundant life You have given me. Thank you for this amazing gift. I love You. Amen.

I am a Temple

"Don't you realize that your body is the temple of the Holy Spirit, who lives in you and was given to you by God? You do not belong to yourself, for God bought you with a high price. So you must honor God with your body." 1 Corinthians 6:19-20 (NLT)

The temple in the Old Testament was the place where all God's people came to worship Him. It was a reverent place, where God's presence was and where God's people could come connect with Him. Inside the temple, was a room called the Holy of Holies where only the Head Priest could come once a year to make atonement for the people's sins. There was a veil separating the inner room from the rest of the temple that was said to be as tall as thirty feet, four inches thick, and take three hundred men to lift it.[8]

When Jesus arose from the dead, the Bible tells us this same curtain that separated God from man was split in two from top to bottom, making a way for us to enter His throne room (Matthew 27:51). Before His ascension, Jesus promised He would leave someone in His place to be His disciples' guide and comforter: the Holy Spirit, God's own Spirit who raised Jesus from the dead. That Spirit now lives in every follower of Jesus (Romans 8:11). And as Paul wrote in 1 Corinthians 6, we are now the Holy Spirit's dwelling place—we are *each* His temple.

"Therefore, brothers and sisters, since we have confidence to enter the holy places by the blood of Jesus, by the new and living way that he opened for us through the curtain, that is, through his flesh" Hebrews 10:19-20

We are His temple, the place where He resides. The Holy of Holies is now in us. That's hard to wrap my mind around. But that's also why Paul says we do not belong to ourselves and must honor God with our bodies. That means honoring our bodies with our minds and actions as well.

Our bodies are God's dwelling place. We need to respect them and say respectful things about them. That means taking care of them by eating healthily and exercising appropriately, not watching or listening to ungodly messages, and being careful about what we take in and put out through our words. Our self-talk matters to God. And, thankfully, the Holy Spirit will help us with this. He will mold us into temples that reflect His glory. And one day, when Jesus returns, our bodies will be made new and glorious. There will be no more pain, no more disabilities, no more shame. What remains will be only wonderful, beautiful, glorious heavenly bodies.

Challenge: Read Ephesians 5:1-21 and meditate on how we as believers are to speak, think, and act. This is just one passage of several throughout the New Testament that gives us such directions. Reflect and pray through the passage, focusing on how to honor God with your body.

Prayer: Thank You, God, for tearing the veil of separation when Jesus died on the cross. Thank You that Your Spirit now resides in me. Let my words, thoughts, actions, and will reflect this awesome truth. Help me to use my body for Your glory alone. Amen.

I am holy

"For you are a people holy to the Lord your God. The Lord your God has chosen you to be a people for His treasured possession, out of all the peoples who are on the face of the earth" Deuteronomy 7:6

What does it mean to be holy? The dictionary tells us it means *sacred* or *spiritually excellent*. We can see that God is considered the Most Holy One. Scripture shows us what is happening in heaven around His throne: the angels never cease singing of His holiness as they stand in His holy presence. We can also see that God has chosen us to be holy (1 Peter 2:9). But what does that mean exactly?

"Holy, holy, holy, is the Lord God Almighty, who was and is and is to come!" Revelation 4:8b

I once heard it described as this: we were created to be *set apart* from the rest of the world, just as the Israelites, God's chosen people were meant to be separate from the surrounding nations. The Israelites were given many laws just so they could be in God's presence. Some of these laws sound really strange to us now, like not being able to eat bacon. However, research says this law may have been given because many diseases are found in eating pork[9]. There are a lot of other laws like this if you read through the first five books of the Bible.

Though they were meant to follow all these laws, they could not hold to them. So, there was a way for them to be forgiven. Leviticus 16 tells us about the scapegoat God provided for His people. The head priest would lay his hands on the goat and pray that all the people's sins would be put on this animal. Does this sound familiar to you? Jesus did the same for us. He took all of our sins upon Himself willingly.

"He is the propitiation for our sins, and not only for ours but also for the sins of the whole world." 1 John 2:2

We are made holy now because of Jesus' death and resurrection. We can be in God's presence in a way that the Israelites had to work hard to achieve – and all because of Jesus. God calls us to be holy, to be separated from the world in which we live. We are not meant to take this gift of salvation and life Jesus has given us and live as the world lives. We are meant to stand out, shining as lights in this dark place.

Challenge: Read 1 Peter 1:13-25 and reflect on what it means to be holy. Does your life look any different than the unbelievers you know? What could you do today to choose holiness?

Prayer: Thank You, Jesus, for being our scapegoat. Thank You for making a way for me to be holy, so I can be in the Father's presence. Thank You for this life and salvation You have given so freely. Please help me choose holiness today. I love You. Amen.

Journal

Part VI

I am a good thing

"So God created mankind in his own image, in the image of God he created them; male and female he created them… God saw all that he had made, and behold, it was very good."

Genesis 1:27, 31

I am a good thing

"So God created mankind in his own image, in the image of God he created them; male and female he created them… God saw all that he had made, and behold, it was very good." Genesis 1:27, 31

Very good. Not just good—very good. Have you ever tasted a decadent dessert? Like maybe a dark chocolate mousse pie or a raspberry cheesecake? Mmmm. I'm salivating just thinking about them. Or perhaps you're a salty or spicy kind of gal. You would rather have a plate of really salty chips or your mom's famous jollof rice. Either way, we know when something is more than good or okay. Something that doesn't just come around every ordinary day.

That is what God said about us when we were made. I have read Genesis 1 more times than I can count, and yet, not until I was writing this did I realize that God uses the term "very" only after he made humans. On every other day – after He had made the heavens and the earth, the angels, the seas and mountains, the birds and fish and other animals – He said what He had made was good (Genesis 1:4,10,12,18,21,25). Only after He created man and woman in His image, completing His creation, did He use the term very good (Genesis 1:31).

"Let all the earth fear the Lord; let all the inhabitants of the world stand in awe of Him! For He spoke, and it came to be; He commanded, and it stood firm." Psalm 33:6-7

Look up the most beautiful landscape pictures in the world, and you'll be mesmerized. God's creation is breathtaking! I have had the opportunity to travel, and my favorite places have been where a picture cannot even capture the brilliance of the view. It is like all you can think is *wow*. You cannot help but stand in awe of the God who created all of it. And yet, God Himself, the Creator, called you and me His very best. He made those mountains and glaciers and sunsets and said good. He made you and said very good. Can you even wrap your mind around that?

Challenge: Take a minute to let this truth sink in: You are God's very good creation. You are so precious to Him. Be still before Him and meditate on how much He loves you.

Prayer: Wow, Jesus. Thank You for revealing this truth to me today – that you made us and said very good. Thank You for that tiny extra word that makes all the difference. Please help me grasp just a little bit more of how much you love me. I love You. Amen.

I am being made beautiful

"He has made everything beautiful in its time." Ecclesiastes 3:11

Did you know that a pearl is formed from an oyster, mussel, or clam[10]? When a parasite works its way into the clam, the clam produces a coat used to irritate the parasite. Layers form, and in time, a pearl is formed. That ugly, slimy clam becomes something beautiful and expensive.

I am not saying you're an ugly duckling that becomes beautiful. We have already established that we are wonderfully and beautifully made. But don't you think about how messed up you are sometimes? I do. Sometimes, I wonder how God could keep loving me when I mess up so often. Sometimes, I think my heart must look ugly to God. But that's the thing. Even though God hates sin and hates that we choose to sin against Him, He is turning our sinful hearts to Him day by day. He is making our dirty, sin-loving hearts and cleaning them, making them pure and holy – like Himself.

"For God knew his people in advance, and he chose them to become like his Son, so that his Son would be the firstborn among many brothers and sisters." Romans 8:29 (NLT)

God chose you and I to become like His Son, holy and blameless. We are beautiful and pure before Him. It is a process. It does not come right away but will take a lifetime – literally. And it is not always easy. Most of the time, it is hard and painful. Much like that parasite must be to the clam. I don't know about you, but I would be resentful if a little parasite came knocking on my door, taking up space in my home and rubbing up against me night and day. No wonder they try to protect themselves with slime. Ew. But really, the same happens with us. Becoming like Jesus is not easy. Sometimes, it seems impossible. But the beautiful thing is that it's not up to us – God is doing the work in us. And He will continue until we are beautiful and like Him completely.

"God will make this happen, for He who calls you is faithful." 1 Thessalonians 5:24

Challenge: Start a journal and write down how you see God working in your life. In a month, go back and reread what you wrote. Remembering what God has done in your life is very encouraging. It is often not until you walk through something difficult that you can look back and see what God did in and through you.

Prayer: Thank You, Lord, for taking the time to sanctify me. Thank you for not giving up on me. Help me through the parts that will be painful for me. Please help me not give up but persevere through the hard times. I know You are with me no matter what. Thank you. I love You. Amen.

I am whole

"The Lord is my shepherd; I have everything I need." Psalm 23:1 (GNT)

Have you heard the saying, "Find your other half" or, "You're not complete without your other half"? So many movies and books point to this worldview: without a man by your side, you're somehow incomplete. It's supposed to be romantic, I guess, but it's just wrong. It is a lie. You are not incomplete without your "soulmate." You are made whole when you come into a relationship with your Maker.

I have had so many friends buy into the lie that "When I get married, I'll be happy." But marriage won't bring you happiness, and it won't make you whole. Your weaknesses in your singleness will remain when you get into a relationship. In fact, they will probably be magnified.

So many of us have probably thought this way when thinking about something, though. If I only had fill-in-the-blank, I'd be happy and whole. But that's not how it works.

"For the joy of the Lord is your strength." Nehemiah 8:10

When the Israelites came out of exile, back to Jerusalem after hundreds of years in Babylon, they longed for the former days when they had a temple - a place for God's presence to dwell. They thought if only they had a temple again, all would be well; they would be happy and whole as a nation. A prophet named Ezra led the people to rebuild the temple, but many of the Israelites cried when it was done, and they were not tears of joy, but of sadness (Ezra 3:12). The temple they thought would usher in God's presence was not the answer. What was missing was their hearts of repentance and willingness to follow the Lord.

So many times, we think if we could __, we would feel complete and happy, but that's a lie from Satan. In reality, Jesus is all we need; we are complete with Him in our lives.

"You, Lord, are all I have, and you give me all I need; my future is in your hands." Psalms 16:5 (GNT)

Challenge: What is that thing or those things you have been wanting lately that you may have believed the lie that if you get __, you'll be happy and whole? Pray about them and give them to God. Surrender your plans and desires to the Father and commit yourself to Him again.

Prayer: Thank You, Lord, for giving me all that I need in Your Presence. In You, I have all that I need. I know You will give me all that I would ever need; I need not fear, only trust You and Your goodness to me. Thank You for Your provision in my life. I give You everything. I love You. Amen.

I am pure

"Blessed are the pure in heart, for they shall see God." Matthew 5:8

What does it mean to be pure in heart? Because I want to see God. I want to see Him moving and working in my life. I want to see His love and His faithfulness every hour of every day. So how can I be pure in my heart? The easy and amazing part is that we are already made pure through Jesus Christ if we have put our hope and trust in Him.

"And from Jesus Christ the faithful witness, the firstborn of the dead, and the ruler of kings on earth. To Him who loves us and has freed us from our sins by His blood." Revelation 1:5

Christ has already freed us from any sins we have committed that would make us impure before Him. Isn't that amazing? We can see God because of what He did for us. Jesus Christ made a way for us to see God by dying on the cross. The other part is up to us, however. We can choose to follow Jesus and live a life of purity, or we can choose to follow the world's ways and live a life of sin. James puts living a life of purity like this: "to keep oneself from being polluted by the world" (1:27). How do we keep ourselves from being polluted by the world? Think about the shows and movies you watch, the songs you listen to, or the friends you hang out with. Are those things pointing you toward Christ, or are they drawing you away from Him? If you say the latter, you may want to think about removing such things from your life because they are polluting your purity. That is a complex statement to think through. Especially when it comes to things you love. But I can tell you it is worth it.

A few years ago, I heard God whisper in my spirit to stop watching *Harry Potter* because He hates witchcraft (see Deuteronomy 18:9-12). Now, I have to say, I was a total fangirl of HP. I read all the books, watched the movies, and visited the Potter World Park at Universal Studios. I loved Harry Potter. But when I heard God ask me, "Ashley, do you love Harry Potter more than *Me*?" I realized my love for this worldly thing was not worth giving up a closer walk with God. So, I gave it up. I gave away all my DVDs and stopped watching them when my friends asked me over for movie nights.

Now, that may seem like a silly example to you. And maybe it is compared to yours. But the reality is that anything that takes our attention away from God will not bring us closer to Him. And those things would be worth giving up. After all, when we pursue pureness, we will see God. And wouldn't that be the most amazing kind of life?

Challenge: List the things in your life that draw you closer to God and that pull you away from God. Challenge yourself to make the first list have more items on it this week and the second list to have fewer. Every week, with discipline, it will get easier. My prayer is that this old hymn will come true in your life: "And the things of the world will grow strangely dim, in the light of His glory and grace[11]."

Prayer: Thank You, Jesus, for making the way for me so I can see God and know You personally. Thank You for revealing the things in my life that have drawn me away from You. Convict my heart when I start pursuing those things and open my eyes to what draws me closer to You. I want to see You, Lord, and know You more. I love You. Amen.

I am godly

"Have nothing to do with irreverent, silly myths. Rather train yourself for godliness; for while bodily training is of some value, godliness is of value in every way, as it holds promise for the present life and also for the life to come." 1 Timothy 4:7-8

Training yourself is hard. Have you ever tried training for a marathon or other sports training? It is no joke. It takes discipline to get up early to run and lift weights. How about sacrificing sleep and rest time to do physical exercise? Nah, I'm good where I am, thank you. The thought of pushing myself until I break isn't really what I live for.

But disciplining ourselves is precisely what God has asked us to do. Not necessarily physically, though caring for our bodies is very important to Him. We should be training ourselves to stay away from thing things that would pollute our minds and souls and instead seek that which is godly.

Godliness means having a devotion to one's purity and holiness. It's choosing the things of God above the things of the world. Sometimes, it's choosing the hard road, the road others don't take because you have to say "no" to things others are doing.

I used to have a really good DVD collection (I know, some of you may not know what a DVD is… Just think old-school Netflix). My favorite movies were rom-coms, and I had a lot. But one day, the Holy Spirit whispered in my ear, "Ashley, you don't need to be watching movies that show premarital sex as *normal*." Woah. Okay, God. But do I have to get rid of my movies? What if I don't watch them? Or what if I watch one or two? It's okay, right?

God was convicting me of my attachment to something that promoted sin. He wanted me to choose between obeying Him or my will. Thankfully, I chose Him that day. At the time, I was dating a pretty awesome guy (now my husband), and I had not realized how those movies affected my thinking. I had the conviction not to kiss any man but my husband, and watching those movies made me covet and lust. I had to choose godliness over my desires. Looking back, I realize that now I don't have the desire to watch those kinds of movies as much. I desire to watch and listen to things that will edify my walk with Christ, not hinder it. It is the process of surrender and discipline that leads to a deeper relationship with Christ.

Challenge: Pray and ask God to reveal any sinful attachment. Challenge yourself – Are you willing to give up sin to pursue godliness? If not, what is standing in your way? Think through these questions as you read 1 Timothy 4.

Prayer: Lord, make me more like You. I surrender my addictions, sin struggles, and anything else that is hindering my growth in godliness. Please open my eyes to how You want to work in my heart. I give You control. Help me let go. Amen.

Part VII

I am adopted

"For all who are led by the Spirit of God are children of God. The Spirit you received does not make you slaves so that you live in fear again; rather, the Spirit you received brought about your adoption to sonship. And by Him we cry, 'Abba, Father.'"

Romans 8:14-15 (NIV)

I am adopted

"For all who are led by the Spirit of God are children of God. The Spirit you received does not make you slaves so that you live in fear again; rather, the Spirit you received brought about your adoption to sonship. And by Him we cry, 'Abba, Father.'" Romans 8:14-15 (NIV)

My mom was adopted. She and her brother were adopted from the hospital as babies, so adoption has always been a part of my vocabulary. I remember when my mom told me she was adopted, I was surprised because she looked like my grandma and grandpa; she acted like them; she was a part of their family in every sense of the word. And that is what adoption is – Being grafted into a family as if you had always been a part of it. In many cultures, there is a taboo around the topic of adoption. It doesn't really happen. In others, there is a sense of wrongness when it comes to transracial adoption. In some cultures, though, adoption is a normal part of society. Adoption is a main part of God's Kingdom. Everyone is welcome and no one is excluded. All races, genders, personalities, professions, and ages are welcome to be grafted into God's family.

"But now that faith has come, we are no longer under a guardian, for in Christ Jesus you are all [children] of God, through faith... There is neither Jew nor Greek, there is neither slave nor free, there is no male and female, for you are all one in Christ Jesus." Galatians 3:25-28

We are children of God, and He is our Father. That is the most intimate relationship you can get. He is our dad. He cares for us and loves us no matter what we do. He knows what is best for us and works everything out for our good (Romans 8:28). Some of us may not have a good example of a dad in our lives, and if that is you, I'm so sorry. Our Father in Heaven is so much better than even the best of dads here on earth, though. We can trust Him completely, and He will never let us down. He will always have our back.

I have a close friend who adopted two toddlers a few years ago. She recently told our Bible Study group that she doesn't even think about her kids being adopted because they're *her* kids. I love that sentiment because it reminds me of how God looks at you and me. We are *His* kids. And He loves us as His own. Adoption is a beautiful picture of God's goodness to us. Though once in slavery and darkness and sin, now we are not only children to the One True King, we are His heirs, His inheritors, and His daughters whom He loves. He is our Father, the One who has our backs, cheers for us, and provides for us more than any earthly father ever could.

Challenge: Write a thank you letter to your Dad in heaven. Thank Him for always having your back and for never disappointing you. Tell Him what is on your mind and in your heart. Then, wait for His response to you.

Prayer: Thank You, Father, for always being there for me. Thank You for calling me your daughter. Thank You for adopting me as your own. Please help me remember this truth as I go about my day. Help me remember I have a Dad who cares about me more than anything. I love You. Amen.

I am chosen

"Even before He made the world, God loved us and chose us in Christ to be holy and without fault in His eyes." Ephesians 1:4 (NLT)

It feels horrible not to be chosen, doesn't it? I have been passed over many times in my life. I was told I wasn't good enough when I tried out for the high school tennis team. When I applied for the gifted program in middle school, I was told I wasn't smart enough. In high school and college, the boys I liked always chose other girls who were more talkative or more outgoing to take to the dances.

I let the opinions of others rule my life for a long time. When I wasn't chosen, I felt the sting deep within me, and I started taking on some of the identities I thought fit better. Maybe I wasn't good enough at anything. Maybe I was dumb. Perhaps I was too shy and, therefore, someone that no one could ever love.

Then, one day, Jesus met me where I was and showed me the truth. I was chosen. Before time began. He chose me to be His daughter, a beautiful, amazing young woman with all these strengths and weaknesses. And He chose you, too.

"Blessed be the God and Father of our Lord Jesus Christ, who has blessed us in Christ with every spiritual blessing in the heavenly places, even as he chose us in him before the foundation of the world, that we should be holy and blameless before him."
Ephesians 1:3-4

You are not a mistake. You are chosen. By the King of Kings who knows everything about everyone, He picked you. Don't ever let the opinion of others rule over what God says about you. I did that for too long and wasted my energy on lies. Please don't make the same mistake as me. It took me years to accept myself and who God created me to be.

If you are where I was – unsure and feeling unwanted, try asking God what He thinks about you. Do some research in His Word – what did He write about who you are to Him? Search for *identity in Christ* and see what verses pop up. Start a journal and listen to what the Holy Spirit whispers to you. Listen to worship music and let the words resonate within your soul. It will take time, but He will speak to and change you from the inside out. And when you can live and think as a chosen daughter of the King, your life will be so much richer.

Challenge: Look up "identity in Christ" in a concordance. Take note of what the Bible has to say about your identity. Spend time praying over these verses and ask God to reveal any lies you may have been believing about yourself.

Prayer: Lord, I thank You for choosing me before time began. O, how You love me, Lord! Thank You for your love and kindness. Please help me live as a daughter who the King chooses. I love You. Amen.

I am grafted in

"I am the true vine, and my Father is the vine dresser. Every branch in me that does not bear fruit he takes away, and every branch that does bear fruit he prunes, that it may bear more fruit." John 15:1-2

There are a lot of plant references throughout Scripture. I, myself, am not a green thumb, as they say. My husband loves giving me plants and beautiful flowers, but I have a hard time keeping them alive. I either water them too much or too little and after a couple of weeks, we have rotting foliage on our coffee table.

Thankfully, our Vine dresser does not treat us as I treat my plants. He knows exactly what we need, exactly when we need it, because He is completely sovereign. Metaphorically speaking, we do not need to worry about how much sun, water, or healthy air we are getting because not only does our vine dresser take care of us, but the Vine to which we are connected is Jesus Himself. The rest of John 15 tells us that when we stay connected to Jesus as the Root of all we say and do, we will bear much fruit and be satisfied.

"Behind and underneath all this there is a holy, God-planted, God-tended root. If the primary root of the tree is holy, there's bound to be some holy fruit. Some of the tree's branches were pruned and you wild olive shoots were grafted in. Yet the fact that

you are now fed by that rich and holy root gives you no cause to gloat over the pruned branches. Remember, you aren't feeding the root; the root is feeding you." Romans 11:17-18 (MSG)

When fruit trees are grafted together, the two trees become one new tree, usually with the best characteristics of both original trees. For example, did you know that back in the 1800s, someone grafted two apple trees together to create a new kind of apple[12]? The Macintosh Apple is now among the most well-liked apples in the world. (Also, the most popular because who does not know Macintosh computers?).

It is the same for us. Jesus, through His death and resurrection, made a way for us to be grafted into His family. In the Old Testament, it was the Israelites who were the chosen people of God, but now, we, too, are His chosen ones. As we are grafted in, we not only join the family of believers, but our root becomes Christ, and we are slowly but surely changed into a new creation (2 Corinthians 5:17), that will be able to bear fruit that will last (John 15:16).

Challenge: Watch a video about how gardeners graft trees together - it is fascinating to watch! Reflect on how the grafting process relates to the Scriptures we have read today.

Prayer: Thank You, Jesus, for making a way for me to be grafted into your family. Thank You for giving me constant access to You, who will enable me to bear much fruit. Let me always be connected to You. Thank You for choosing me. I love You. Amen.

I am safe

"Those who live in the shelter of the Most High will find rest in the shadow of the Almighty. This I declare about the Lord: He alone is my refuge, my place of safety; He is my God, and I trust Him." Psalm 91:1-2 (NLT)

I used to be a very fearful child. I was afraid of many, many things. I wouldn't talk in elementary school because I feared my teachers. I wouldn't go on grand adventures with my sisters in our backyard because I was scared of getting hurt. One year, I was so afraid of our house catching fire that I slept on my parents' bedroom floor for months. I was terrified.

I want to say that I naturally grew out of this fear when I reached middle school, but unfortunately, that wasn't the case. My worries just turned into other things: fear of rejection, fear of unpopularity, fear of death, fear of loneliness. The list goes on.

My mom taught me a song to sing when some of these fears assaulted me at night. Maybe you've heard it: "When I am afraid, I will trust in You, I will trust in You, I will trust in You." I would sing this over and over to myself in my room with the nightlight on, trying to go to sleep. (Oh yeah, I was afraid of the dark, too.)

The amazing thing about fear, I learned later, is that it's a mind thing. When I focus on my worries, they somehow get bigger and bigger. Thankfully, the opposite happens when we focus on Jesus – the fear lessens. It goes away, even. When our eyes are fixed on the One who holds our lives, loves us, and is working on our behalf, everything else fades away, and we are left with peace.

"There is no fear in love, but perfect love casts out fear. For fear has to do with punishment, and whoever fears has not been perfected in love." 1 John 4:18

Perfect love is Jesus. Jesus casts out our fear. And when we trust Him, He hides us under the shadow of His arms. He is our safe place. No matter what happens, we are safe if we abide in our Father – the Sovereign One in true control. He may not divert our problems, but He will keep us safe in the midst of them.

Challenge: Write out what you are afraid of. Name them. Then, either burn the paper or tear It up and throw it away. Pray and ask God to give you peace instead. Read Psalm 91 and try memorizing some of the verses. Next time you are afraid, remember those verses and put your trust in Him. In Him, we are safe.

Prayer: Thank You, Jesus, for being my safe place. Thank You for casting out the fear in me. Help me to focus on You instead of my fear. Help me to trust in You. I love You. Amen.

I am one who lacks nothing

*Y*ou are one who lacks nothing.

This truth is really hard to believe, isn't it? If I only had _____, I would be happy. If I were more like _____, my life would be so much better. Aren't these the thoughts that often go through our minds?

"The Lord is my Shepherd; I lack nothing.
He makes me lie down in green pastures,
He leads me beside quiet waters,
He refreshed my soul.
He guides me along the right paths
for His name's sake.
Even though I walk through the darkest valley,
I will fear no evil,
for You are with me;
Your rod and Your staff,
they comfort me." Psalm 23:1-4 (NIV)

I love this psalm. Isn't it so calming? The first line sticks out, though. "The Lord is my Shepherd, I lack nothing." Really – nothing? Is that even possible?

The more I scroll through Instagram, or whatever social media app is out there nowadays, the more I think I'm missing something. After all, my life doesn't look like *hers*. My house isn't as cute as *theirs*. I want a body like *hers*. I wish I could go on *that* vacation. The list goes on. But when we do that, we have fallen into the comparison trap. The comparison trap is a lonely, horrible place to be. No one quite understands – Everyone else's lives are better than our own. At least, that is what we think when we're in the trap.

But that could not be further from the truth, dear friends! We have *all we need* in Christ! When you and I start comparing, we switch our eyes to what we don't have instead of thanking God for all we do have. We have freedom in Christ. We have unconditional love. We have divine favor. We have irresistible grace. And the list goes on!

"But whatever gain I had, I counted as loss for the sake of Christ. Indeed, I count everything as loss because of the surpassing worth of knowing Christ Jesus my Lord. For his sake I have suffered the loss of all things and count them as rubbish, in order that I may gain Christ." Philippians 3:7-8

Challenge: Next time you catch yourself in the comparison trap, try to stop and list ten things you are thankful for.

Prayer: Lord, forgive me for constantly comparing myself with others. Help me choose thankfulness for what You have given me already. Thank You that I lack nothing. Help me believe it. I love You. Amen

Journal

Part VIII

I am anointed

"But you have been anointed by the Holy One, and you all have knowledge."

1 John 2:20

I am anointed

"But you have been anointed by the Holy One, and you all have knowledge." 1 John 2:20

You may not know what anointing is unless you grew up in the Pentecostal Church. I had never heard of pastors anointing people with oil until I moved to Ghana. Maybe that was just my experience growing up in a suburban American Baptist church, but the first time I saw the pastor call up people to be anointed for healing, I was pretty skeptical.

To anoint means literally to smear with oil[13]. In the Bible, many references exist to the priests anointing the holy objects with oil. The priests themselves also had to be anointed before entering the temple. It was a way to proclaim something or someone was holy. In the New Testament, Jesus was anointed with a special perfume before His death, signifying He was the Anointed One, the one the Jews had been waiting for since the garden, the Messiah. After Christ's ascension, the disciples tell the other believers we are all now anointed because of Jesus. As John Piper puts it: "Jesus has poured out on every Christian something of his own anointing from the Father[14]."

"And it is God who establishes us with you in Christ, and has anointed us, and who has also put his seal on us and given us his Spirit in our hearts as a guarantee." 2 Corinthians 1:21-22

As Christians or Christ followers, we have been anointed by God to be holy, set apart from the world, and do God's work while we're here. And one day, because of Jesus and His Spirit's presence in our hearts as a guarantee, we will live with Him forever in paradise. Until then, we are to act as God's anointed ones – sharing His love with those around us. We are not to conform to the ways of our world (Romans 12:1), but to follow Jesus' ways of counter-cultural love, forgiveness, power, justice, and truth.

Challenge: Spend time praying over your life and your future. Ask God to start revealing what He has anointed you for. The first step for us is surrender. Are you willing to say "Yes, Lord" no matter what, where, or to whom He calls you? If not, ask God to soften your heart until you are.

Prayer: Lord, thank You for anointing me. Thank You for putting Your Spirit in me as a guarantee. I believe You have created me for a purpose; please lead me in that purpose for Your Name's sake. Guide me to the place and the people where You would anoint me. Do not pass over me, Lord. I love You. Amen.

I am equipped

"Now may the God of peace who brought again from the dead our Lord Jesus, the great shepherd of the sheep, by the blood of the eternal covenant, equip you with everything good that you may do his will, working in us that which is pleasing in his sight, through Jesus Christ, to whom be glory forever and ever. Amen."
Hebrews 13:20-21

Have you ever been assigned to a project or role and knew you would probably fail because the task seemed so insurmountable? I know a young girl who was asked to play a vital role in human history, and she also thought she was unqualified. She was just a teenager when the angel visited her chambers. She wasn't even married yet, which back in the day meant she wasn't worth much in society's eyes. But God chose her to be the mother of Jesus, His only Son.

Do you think Mary felt qualified for such a role? I bet she was terrified. But her answer to God is one of submission. Mary knew that God would equip her in every way she needed to be a good mother to the Messiah.

In my life, I can tell you that I have done so many things that I thought I could never do. One time, I felt the Holy Spirit's nudging to lead a workshop at my church. I presented on a topic I was passionate about, but to a room full of strangers, many of whom were experts in the field. I felt like I was under-equipped for the role, but I said yes, listening to the prompting of the Holy Spirit. Throughout the presentation, my hand tremors, a hereditary gift that acts up when I'm nervous, were miraculously gone for the entire presentation! (That was a big deal for me because these hand tremors have caused me many embarrassing moments throughout the years.) God asked me to do something, and He equipped me to do it.

That is what God does. He has done it with Mary; He's done it with me, and He'll do it for you. Is God asking you to do something scary that you think you could not possibly do? Do not let fear get in the way of an opportunity for God to show how He can equip you for anything and everything. Who knows what these opportunities will lead to?

Challenge: Read Luke 1-2. I know it is the "Christmas story," but we can read it anytime. Focus on Mary's responses and actions. What did she ask the angel? What did she do? How did she respond overall? How does her response challenge your responses to God?

Prayer: Lord, thank You for not leaving me without support and help. Thank You for allowing us the opportunity to do amazing things, though sometimes difficult. Thank You for not leaving us where we are but guiding me and shaping me into a woman after Your own heart. I love You, Jesus. Amen.

I am purposed

"The plans of the Lord stand firm forever, the purposes of His heart through all generations." Psalm 33:11

When I taught middle school, I learned a trick for placing students in small groups to do a project of some sort. You hear the horror stories of students who get trapped doing all the work on an assignment while their partners sit back and relax while "earning" the A they don't deserve. To try and get around this, I gave jobs to each group member. Each person in the group had a specific role to play, and each role was vital to the outcome of the project. I found I was able to grade each student with more accuracy. I also found that there was more peace within the groups because they knew their purpose and could give their all to fulfill it.

God, too, has given each of us a specific purpose. Every person on this planet has a purpose designed by God from the beginning of time, all for His glory and all for our good. It is kind of crazy to think about, but it is true. And much like the peace my students found when they focused on their task, we also can experience peace when we know our purpose and walk in it.

Here, you might ask, but what if I don't know my purpose? That is okay. God will reveal what He wants from you when you and all the circumstances are ready, and not until then. Purposes may also grow and change in your life, and that is okay, too. When I was sixteen, God called me to missions, though I didn't know what that meant then. It was not until I was twenty-six that He finally revealed what that meant – I was to move to Ghana to teach after ten years of waiting. I did not just sit on my hands and wait, though. I grew in my relationship with God and others; I finished my education and got a job; I continued praying for direction and guidance; I obeyed when He gave me direction. I also longed for more many times throughout those years, but I waited on His timing. And oh, was it worth it.

"The Lord has made everything for its own purpose" Proverbs 16:4 (NASB)

For sure, God has purposed us to follow Him. We are to worship and adore Him, to love others with abandon, to be generous and kind, and to share His love with others. For now, do those things. And pray for direction as to what He wants for your future. He will guide you in your purpose in His good timing.

Challenge: Choose a Christian biography to read. There are so many good ones: Elizabeth Elliot, Harriett Tubman, and Corrie Ten Boom, to name a few. Reflect on the purpose God laid out for them and their response of obedience. Ask God to reveal your purpose in His good timing.

Prayer: Thank You, God, for creating me with a unique purpose. Thank You for revealing it to me in Your good timing. I pray that I will follow You and serve others as I wait. I ask that You work through me as I live for You. Help me show others what it means to follow You. I love You. Amen.

I am salt & light

"You are the salt of the earth, but if salt has lost its taste, how shall its saltiness be restored? It is no longer good for anything except to be thrown out and trampled under people's feet... You are the light of the world... Let your light shine before others, so that they may see your good works and give glory to your Father who is in heaven."
Matthew 5:13-14, 16

I love salt. My husband usually tells me I am being unhealthy with how much salt I like to pour on my popcorn, yam chips, turkey... You name it. I love salty snacks! Did you know the true purpose of salt back in the day was two-fold? One of its purposes was for taste. Who wants to eat bland potatoes? The other, though, was for preservative purposes. This was when people didn't have freezers or refrigerators and had to salt their meats and vegetables, so they didn't go bad.

When Jesus referred to his disciples as the salt and light of the earth, He knew His followers would be well-versed in the purposes of both light and salt. They knew light was so important as the sun set before dinnertime in the winter months[15]. To see their dinner and get around at night (remember, this was before electricity), they had to use lamps. If they had put the light under the basket, it would have done them no good.

They also knew that salt that lost its saltiness would have to be thrown out (Matthew 5:13). If the salt was not used for preserving their food, seasoning, or even sometimes as a disinfectant, why bother with it?

In the same way, Jesus was encouraging His disciples to embrace their calling and purpose. They were to be the light of the world, the salt in their communities. They were to shine God's goodness and love so much that others could be guided by their light. They were to live so much in contrast to the world that if they stopped or hid their light, people would notice because it would be complete darkness.

Their lives of submission and service to God were to be so different than the bland life of those following the pleasures of this age.

"By this, all people will know that you are my disciples if you have love for one another." John 13:35

Jesus is calling you and me to be the same. To be the light that shines for Christ. To be the tasty and enduring salt to your neighbors and friends. Do not be afraid to shine that light. The God of the universe has got you. He will not let your light go out if you follow Him.

Challenge: Who do you know that is currently living in darkness? They're stuck in depression or anxiety. Perhaps you know someone who is struggling with an addiction or another sin. Pray for them now. Ask God one way you can show them His love today.

Maybe it's an encouraging text message or a call. Perhaps He will ask you to share your testimony with them. Be open to how God wants you to shine your light to those around you.

Prayer: Jesus, how can I ever thank You enough? Thank You for being the light of the world and the salt of the earth. I want to follow You more. I want to be Your hands and feet to the people You have placed in my life. Please help me shine this light and be the salt to others I meet today. Let fear not get in the way of my obedience to You. I love You. Amen.

I am a builder

Read The Parable of the Talents found in Matthew 25:14-30. Have you ever been so overwhelmed that you curled up in a ball and shut out the world? I find comfort by hiding under my oversized, cozy comforter, reading, or watching a movie. However you shut out the world, we all have those tendencies to run and hide when things get to be too much. I remember one time, I had just been informed about the horrors of human trafficking happening in my neighborhood. I felt so overwhelmed that such a horrific thing was happening, and I felt like I didn't know what I could do to stop it. So, I hid. I pretended like I had not just learned that thousands of girls and boys were stolen by promises of education and love and, instead, forced to do unspeakable acts for grown men and women who bought them. I binged Netflix. I ate pizza. I did nothing.

This reminded me of a parable Jesus told his disciples. One day the Master gave some money to three different employees. Each one invested the money in some way, except the last one. He buried the money in the sand and waited. When the Master returned, He praised the other two for doing something with the things He had entrusted to them. But the last one, he scolded, asking, "If you knew I was after the best, why did you do less than the least?" (Matthew 25:26 MSG).

Yikes. When I was doing nothing with the information I was given – that was me burying my head in the sand just as the foolish man buried his treasure in the sand. I let my fear stop me from attempting to do anything. God does not like this attitude, so I fixed it. I ended up telling others about the atrocities happening and am still telling others today. Sure, it is not much – I may not be breaking down doors to save these kids, but at least I'm doing something with the tools and influence God has given me.

"And walk in love, as Christ loved us and gave himself up for us, a fragrant offering and sacrifice to God." Ephesians 5:2

Would you believe me if I told you that you have influence in your corner, too? God put you in your home, school, workplace, and friend group for a reason. How are you using the resources, time, and knowledge God has entrusted to you? I would encourage you to learn from my mistake and not make a habit of burying your head in the sand. Don't worry; God will help you build His Kingdom well. All we have to do is show up, ready to do *something*.

Challenge: Do something today to build God's Kingdom a little bit. That could be helping your neighbor water her plants or making cookies for your friends. It could be writing a thank you note for your teachers or washing the dishes for your mom. Acts of kindness show others they are valued and worth it.

Prayer: Thank You for the ability to do something today. Thank You for the opportunity You have given me to work alongside You to build Your Kingdom here. Open my eyes to the ways I can show love and kindness to others today. Help me use my gifts and talents as an investment to make this world a better place. I love You. Amen.

Journal

Part IX

I am appointed

"You did not choose me, but I chose you and appointed you that you should go and bear fruit and that your fruit should abide, so that whatever you ask the Father in my name, He may give it to you."

John 15:16

I am appointed

"You did not choose me, but I chose you and appointed you that you should go and bear fruit and that your fruit should abide, so that whatever you ask the Father in my name, He may give it to you." John 15:16

The definition of appointed is to be designated for a specific task. Deborah was one of Israel's judges before they had kings to rule them. She is the only woman judge mentioned in the Bible, and let's be honest, in Bible times, women were often overlooked and thought of as less than men. So, for Deborah to be appointed judge in all the land – that was rare! Not only was she a wise and just ruler, but she also went into battle with her men and conquered the enemy. (You can read her whole story in Judges 4-5).

When Deborah was appointed Judge of Israel, I bet she didn't know what she was getting herself into. How could she have known that their enemies would rise against them, and she would be asked to give up everything to defend her people? But Deborah knew it was not the Israelite people who had appointed her, but God. She understood that when God appointed her to be judge, He would also equip her to be able to do what needed to be done.

The same is true for us. Notice the command following our appointment in John 15:16. Jesus appoints us and then commands us to go and bear fruit that will last. The fruit Jesus is referring to is not planting a mango tree; rather He is referring to showing the fruits of the Holy Spirit.

"But the fruit of the Spirit is love, joy, peace, patience, kindness, goodness, faithfulness, gentleness, self-control; against such things there is no law." Galatians 5:22-23

When we bear these attributes – love, joy, peace, patience, kindness, goodness, faithfulness, gentleness, and self-control – others will see God in us. And we will fulfill God's appointment for us when we obey Him this way.

Challenge: Think through the fruits of the spirit listed above, and list practical ways you have done each in the past week. For example, maybe you were patient in traffic, or perhaps you were kind to someone who didn't deserve it. Which fruit do you tend to practice the most? The least? Reflect on other ways you can show the fruit this week.

Prayer: Lord, thank You for appointing me to go and bear fruit. Help me bear fruit that will last. Thank You for equipping me with Your Holy Spirit and revealing ways I can serve others through bearing these fruits. Please reveal to me ways I can put these fruits into practice this week. I love You. Amen.

I am a living sacrifice

"Therefore, I urge you, brothers and sisters, in view of God's mercy, to offer your bodies as a living sacrifice, holy and pleasing to God— this is your true and proper worship. Do not conform to the pattern of this world, but be transformed by the renewing of your mind. Then you will be able to test and approve what God's will is—His good, pleasing, and perfect will." Romans 12:1-2 (NIV)

In the Old Testament, before Jesus became our once-for-all sacrifice, ensuring our salvation for all time, animals had to be sacrificed on an altar to bring propitiation for the people's sins. For a person to be right before God, to even be in His presence, they had to sacrifice a ram, goat, or lamb - or a bird if someone could not afford the others. Blood had to be spilled on their behalf to take away their sins.

These sacrifices were such a part of not only the Jewish tradition but also pagan rituals to the idols of the time that when Paul wrote to the Romans about being a living sacrifice, many would not have questioned what that meant. To sacrifice is to give something up. To *be* a sacrifice is to give yourself up. To stand on the altar and give your life to Christ. To be a *living* sacrifice is to put yourself in God's hands daily, over and over again.

Animals are not the most willing creatures, especially birds, rams, goats, and lambs. Don't you think these animals would have strayed a few times? They might have gotten off the altar and wandered nearby to find something to eat—the same with us as living sacrifices. We will most likely stray a few times. We may stumble and mess up and outright fail. But are we willing to humble ourselves and return to the altar of grace? Are we willing to surrender again after we mess up for the umpteenth time? When we do, we show God we love and value Him. "This is our true and proper worship" (Romans 12:1b).

Paul continues in verse 2 to show us practical ways to surrender our lives to Christ: First, we are to transform our thinking to match Christ, and second, we are to follow God's will. Neither is easy, and we will probably fail a thousand times trying to do them, but both are important to our walk with Christ. May God continue to transform your mind and your will to imitate His - for your good and for His glory.

Challenge: Read through Leviticus 1 and use your senses to imagine what it would have been like to sacrifice animals – What would it look like? What would you smell? What would you hear? What would you feel? Then, think about the cross on which Jesus sacrificed His life once and for all. Go through the same questions as above. Spend time thinking, imagining, and praying.

Prayer: Thank You, Jesus, for being our sacrifice! How can I thank You enough? Thank You for removing the need to sacrifice animals. Please help me learn what it means to give up my life as a living sacrifice for You. Help me surrender the things I have held onto, unwilling to let You interfere. Forgive me, Father. Help me submit daily to Your will so that I may live a wonderful and fulfilling life for You. I love You. Amen.

I am part of a chosen people

"But you are a chosen race." 1 Peter 2:9

Have you ever seen or read *Anastasia*? It's a story about a girl who grows up as an orphan, always feeling alone and abused. One day, her life changed. She finds out she is a princess! Imagine living your whole life thinking you are alone, unwanted, and unworthy of love and then finding out you are adored, treasured, and influential.

That story hits home because I once felt that way, too. *Did anyone really care about me? Why did I always feel like such a loser?* But God so graciously reached into my doubts, brushed them away with His love, and taught me to think differently about myself. I had to learn to think differently, not as the world had taught me – always to compare myself, never to be enough – but as my Father teaches me through His Word – I am enough in Christ Jesus (2 Corinthians 3:8); I am loved with an everlasting love (Jeremiah 31:3). And I am part of His chosen people.

"For you are a people holy to the LORD your God. The LORD your God has chosen you to be a people for his treasured possession out of all the peoples who are on the face of the earth."
Deuteronomy 7:6

Not only are you and I chosen, but we are a part of His chosen people. A group that has been signaled out from before time began to be holy and set apart for God's purposes and glory. It started with the Israelites, Abraham's descendants, and now reached out to all who believe Jesus is the Son of God (Romans 11).

Being a part of the group means we are a part of something bigger than ourselves and our small circle. This group has lasted generations upon generations, with millions of people from all different ethnicities, backgrounds, and geographical locations. God's chosen people. We are a part of this group. Let us be intentional, then, to live like we are God's chosen people.

Challenge: List ten people in your church, family, or friend circle. Then, spend time praying for each one. You could pray for all of them today or spend the next week praying for them individually. Let God lead you to what to pray for each person.

Prayer: Thank You, Lord, for choosing me before time began to be a part of Your chosen people. Thank You for making this possible through Jesus' sacrifice. Please help me live out this calling through obedience to Your Words in Scripture. I love You; help me show You my love through my actions. Amen.

I am part of a royal priesthood

"But you are a chosen race, a royal priesthood" 1 Peter 2:9

When I think of a priest, I usually think of men in robes and long crosses around their necks who are a part of the Catholic church. Or I think of a person in a black short-sleeve shirt with a white collar who acts as a pastor. I never think of *myself* as a priest. I don't have a degree in theology, and no church has ordained me. But I am a priest, according to Scripture. And so are you.

Priesthood in the Old Testament was a position that interceded to God on the people's behalf. Aaron, Moses' brother, was chosen as the first priest for the Israelites. His role was to offer sacrifices on behalf of the people – interceding for their sins so they did not have to pay the price – which was death. As time passed, other priests were chosen – all through the Levitical line – each to intercede on the people's behalf so they did not have to face any penalties. As more and more priests became corrupt, the prophets started speaking about one Priest who would come and be our Intercessor once and for all. That Priest is Jesus. Jesus paid the ultimate price, so we are forever pure and forgiven in God's presence. He is our ultimate Intercessor (Romans 8:34).

"First of all, then, I urge that supplications, prayers, intercessions, and thanksgivings be made for all people" 1 Timothy 2:1

Now, as followers of this Great Intercessor, we have also taken up the role as priests. We are intercessors for those who don't believe in Jesus. 1 Timothy says we should be praying for others all the time. It is an essential role for a Christian to follow. As we pray for others, we fulfill the priestly role Jesus has called us into.

Challenge: Watch *The Bible Project's* video on Royal Priesthood. Make a list of people you know who aren't following Jesus. Spend time praying for them.

Prayer: Thank You, Jesus, for being our ultimate Intercessor, for paying the price of Your life so I can have life, too. Thank You for the people You have put in my life who need You. Please open their eyes to see You and to be impacted by Your presence in their lives. Please open my eyes to see ways to pray for them and serve them with Your love. I love You. Amen.

I am part of a holy nation

"But you are a chosen race, a royal priesthood, a holy nation, a people for his own possession, that you may proclaim the excellencies of him who called you out of darkness into his marvelous light." 1 Peter 2:9

One of my favorite parts of teaching at an international school has been the diverse people I have gotten to know. I have had students from over sixty nations in my classroom. How amazing to get to know the different cultures' ways of doing things and thinking about the world. One thing I have had to be careful to do is teach globally, making sure to connect the content to every student's heritage and diverse background. When we have learned about American history, for example, I also bring in other nations' histories. And by doing this, I have discovered there is no perfect nation. All are corrupted and broken.

But there is one nation that is set apart: the nation of believers. Our true nation, whose God is The God. A nation of men, women, and children who profess that Jesus is King and that our lives are purposed to follow Him. A nation with only peace, love, kindness, and goodness. A nation where people go out of their way to love others and provide for those in need. God's nation.

"Blessed is the nation whose God is the LORD, the people whom he has chosen as his heritage!" Psalm 33:12

This nation is yours and mine. We are not of this world as Jesus was not of this world (John 17:16). We belong to a Kingdom that will not perish or be destroyed (Hebrews 12:28). We belong to a Kingdom with a King who will return and make His home with us forever. This is our Kingdom. This is our nation. Isn't it amazing?

Challenge: Spend time meditating on Revelation 21-22, when Jesus will return, and we will be forever with Him in the New Kingdom and Earth. What glorious promises fill these pages! What hope to cling to as the world passes away!

Prayer: Thank you, God, for welcoming me into Your Kingdom, Your Nation that cannot and will not be destroyed. Thank You that I am not of this world, as Jesus was not of this world. Help me live like this is so. Help me trust You when all I see is the brokenness of this world around me. Help me encourage my brothers and sisters to continue trusting and following You until Your return. I love You. Amen.

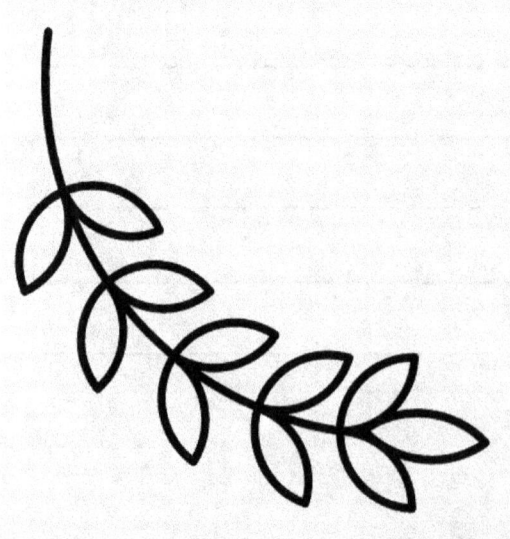

Part X

I am called

"To those who are called, beloved in God the Father and kept for Jesus Christ: May mercy, peace, and love be multiplied to you."

Jude 1:1-2

I am called

"[God has] saved us and called us to a holy calling, not because of our works but because of His own purpose and grace, which He gave us in Christ Jesus before the ages began." 2 Timothy 1:8-9

Throughout Scripture, we see people who were called by God to do extraordinary things. Abraham was called to leave his hometown and take his family to a new land. Moses was called to bring God's people out of slavery in Egypt. Samuel was called when he was just a boy to be a devout prophet who would lead God's people back to Himself. Peter and the other disciples were called by Jesus to follow Him as He did His ministry here on earth.

At each one of these callings, the people could have said no. They could have looked at the insurmountable task in front of them and walked away from God's call. Moses actually did try to walk away. He gave reason after reason as to why God had called the wrong person, but in the end, he chose to surrender to God's calling on his life. And what amazing signs and wonders he got to witness because of his obedience! (See Exodus 3-4, 14.)

I first heard God calling me to follow Him when I was a young child. Throughout my life, I have chosen to follow the Lord step by step, seeking His will and direction for my life. Just as Abraham was told to go to the land God would show Him (Genesis 12:1), most of the time, we don't get the entire map at once. Abraham had to be dependent on God for each step of the journey that would lead him to his new home.

"Trust in the Lord with all your heart, and do not lean on your own understanding. In all your ways acknowledge Him, and He will make straight your paths." Proverbs 3:5-6

It is a daily surrendering of your plans and seeking the Lord to reveal His plans. It is the choice to be dependent on God and not on your own resources. And it is the willingness to accept whatever calling He places on your life. Will you trust Him and follow Him? Will you say yes when He calls you?

Challenge: Choose one of the people mentioned in today's devotion to read about. Focus on how God called them and what directions He gave them in the beginning, as well as their response. Connect their responses to your own response to God – Are you willing to say yes to God no matter the circumstances?

Prayer: Lord Jesus, my God forever, thank You for calling me by name. Thank You for choosing me. Please help me say yes to You when You ask me to do something or go somewhere. Let me be obedient to Your call. I love You. Amen.

I am kept

"To those who are called, beloved in God the Father and kept for Jesus Christ: May mercy, peace, and love be multiplied to you."
Jude 1:1-2

Kept means to hold on to, host fast to, hang on to, or save. When Jude says we are kept for Jesus Christ, he means Jesus has our back. He has got us, so we don't need to worry. We are held safe and sound in His hands, no matter what life may throw our way.

Jesus' disciples learned this while they were following Him. One day, after teaching, Jesus asked his friends to go with Him to the other side of the lake. Jesus had been preaching all day, so He was tired and decided to take a nap. That sounds reasonable, right? Well, a little while later, a big storm picked up when they were probably in the middle of the lake. Mark described it: "The waves were breaking into the boat, so that the boat was already filling" (Mark 4:37). Needless to say, the disciples were terrified. "They woke [Jesus] and said, 'Teacher, do you not care that we are perishing?'" (v. 38). And what did Jesus do? He wakes up, rebukes the wind, and tells the sea to "Be Still" (v. 39).

Have you ever been in a scary situation where you were thinking, "Hello, God, where are you? Why are you sleeping?!" One such time for me was when I was flying in a small plane that had so much turbulence, I thought for sure, we were going down. I prayed the whole time, clutching the seat rests, completely white-knuckled. When we landed, I wanted to kiss the ground. Afterward, I realized that God had had me in His hands the entire flight; I was kept safe by Him.

There's an old hymn that talks about this[16]:

When I fear my faith will fail
Christ will hold me fast
When the tempter would prevail
He will hold me fast

Jesus will hold us fast. We need not fear anything that may happen. He will keep us in His hands forever, so there is genuinely nothing to fear.

Challenge: What are you afraid of? Read Psalms 46 and write down the phrases that show God is in control and we are safe in Him. Reflect on this passage and give God whatever is on your heart today.

Prayer: Jesus, thank You for keeping me. Thank You for not letting me fall. Please remind me of these promises in Psalm 46 whenever I feel afraid. I trust You, Lord. Thank You for Your ever-present hand on me and my life. I love You. Amen.

I am created for a purpose

"For I know the plans I have for you," declares the LORD, "plans to prosper you and not to harm you, plans to give you hope and a future." Jeremiah 29:11 (NIV)

You are created for a purpose. Yes, you. God put you on this earth, in the town you live in, with the family you have, in the time we are in, for a divine purpose. And it is a purpose that only you have.

Our God is such a creative God. He, who made the universe with its many seasons and types of wildlife and landscapes, has also created each of us with different likes, dislikes, passions, spiritual gifts, and talents. All of these things align with our purposes. Isn't it almost incomprehensible?

Think of a suspense movie. From the very beginning, you're hooked to the plot line, on the edge of your seat through every twist and turn, yelling at the person going into the room (Seriously, why do they always go into the creepy room?) - waiting for that moment where it will all make sense. Thankfully, most movies and books end with a happily-ever-after, bird's eye view of what happened and why, and there is usually a neat bow to tie all the clues and missing pieces together.

In real life, we rarely can understand or even begin to grasp everything God is doing in our lives. Scripture tells us that there is meaning to everything (Romans 8:28), and yet, we do not have the capabilities to understand God's purposes for most things that happen in this world (Isaiah 55:8-9). Our thoughts cannot fathom what He has done from beginning to end (Ecclesiastes 3:11).

"I know that You can do all things; no purpose of Yours can be thwarted." Job 42:2

Most of the time if I am being honest, I cannot figure out why certain things are happening the way they are. "How can this be a part of God's plan for my life?" I think. But if I can get around my lack of understanding and choose to trust Him, I can continue to follow the Lord's leading in my life. And even if we mess up or fail – nothing, absolutely nothing can stop God's plans and purposes for our lives. It is impossible for His plans to fail.

Challenge: Let's do some brainstorming and make some lists. Make a list of your passions, likes, hobbies, and talents. Then, make a list of what you think your spiritual gifts are. Looking at these lists, make a list of what types of work you may enjoy doing. Has God led you to believe you should be doing something specific yet? Write those down, too. Pray over your lists and commit your way to the Lord. Remember that God will lead you step by step, so do not worry if you have no idea yet. Keep trusting in His perfect timing.

Prayer: Thank You, Lord, for my purpose. Thank You for creating me with so many unique talents, passions, and gifts. Please reveal what You would have me do and where You would have me go when the time is right. Help me trust You in the meantime. I love You. Amen.

I am created for good works

"For we are his workmanship, created in Christ Jesus for good works, which God prepared beforehand, that we should walk in them." Ephesians 2:10

It has always been easy for me to think about what I could be doing and how I could do so much more. That may come from my talent for comparing myself with others I see on social media. But that kind of mindset gets in the way of the purpose God has put in front of us for today: Love God and love others.

When Jesus was asked what the most important law in all of Scripture was, He replied:

"Love the Lord your God with all your heart and with all your soul and with all your mind and with all your strength… [And] you shall love your neighbor as yourself." Mark 12:30-31

That's it. That is how we show the world our devotion to the Lord – We show love to Him by showing His love to the world. One of the ways we can do this is by doing good works.

Ephesians 2:10 tells us that the good works we do have been prepared by God *beforehand*. Before you were born, God knew whose life you would touch by being hospitable, kind, generous, and loving. He has orchestrated events and people's timelines so that you can meet people who desperately need what you have – God's love. Does it seem a little overwhelming to think about? I know; I get it. But don't become apathetic because you're afraid of messing things up, not doing enough, or failing miserably. Try! Smile at a stranger. Start a conversation. Do a kind thing. Who knows how your act of kindness will lift the person's spirits and change their life?

The best part is that God promised the Holy Spirit would guide us in our good works. You are not alone. God is with you every step of the way. If you listen, you will hear when He whispers in your ear to say "hi" to the stranger, give money to the homeless girl, and stand up against an injustice. God will equip you so you can love others with abandon.

Challenge: List five good works you could do this week. Pray that God will open your eyes to opportunities He puts in your way.

Prayer: Lord, please help me see how I can love others today. Open my eyes to those You have placed in my life who may be hurting, and help me see ways to show them kindness. Thank you for the abundant love You have shown me. Help me point others to this amazing love through my good works. I love You. Amen.

I am fruitful

"You did not choose Me, but I chose you and appointed you that you should go and bear fruit and that your fruit should abide, so that whatever you ask the Father in my name, He may give it to you." John 15:16

Have you ever seen an apple tree where every apple you picked was rotten? Or an orange tree where every orange upon the tree had a worm infestation? Or have you ever seen a Christian who acted any way *but* like Jesus? Someone whose actions did not match what they said they believed?

Sadly, many ex-believers said they left the church because of how the Christians inside acted towards them. History itself shows the sordid past of "Christians" doing ungodly things in the name of Christ – the Crusades, the slave trade, colonialism – I could go on. Jesus was very clear about those who call themselves Christians but are "fruitless", and those who say one thing but act the opposite.

"Yes, I am the vine; you are the branches. Those who remain in me, and I in them, will produce much fruit. For apart from me you can do nothing. Anyone who does not remain in me is thrown away like a useless branch and withers. Such branches are gathered into a pile to be burned." John 15:5-6 (NLT)

Burned. Like in hell. Yikes. It's verses like these that should make us examine our fruitfulness. The key part here, though, is not performance Christianity – doing good works to please God – the critical part is abiding in Jesus. Apart from Him, we can do *nothing*. We cannot produce fruit – good works – without His Presence working in us. When we surrender to Him, His will, and His ways for us, He will lead us in doing the good works He has prepared for us since the beginning of time (Ephesians 2:10). He will work in us, refining us and changing us to look more and more like Him every day (Romans 8:29). He will grow the fruit of the Spirit in our lives (Galatians 5:22).

So don't worry about how much fruit you produce and if it's enough to satisfy God. Focus instead on being with Jesus – abiding in Him – daily walking and talking with Him – seeking Him for direction in everything you do. The rest will follow.

Challenge: Spend time meditating on the verses in today's devotional. Pray and ask God to reveal where you may not be abiding in Him. Surrender those parts to Him, and ask for more fruit, more growth in each part of your life.

Prayer: Thank You, Jesus, for the fruit You have grown in my life. Thank You for leading me in the good works You have prepared beforehand for me to walk in. Thank You for not giving up on me. Forgive me for the times I have talked the talk but not walked in obedience. Let me always abide in You, Jesus, for the rest of my days. Keep me in Your Presence and grow Your fruit in me. I love You. Amen.

Part XI

"There are different kinds of gifts, but the same Spirit distributes them. There are different kinds of service, but the same Lord. There are different kinds of working, but in all of them and in everyone it is the same God at work."

1 Corinthians 12:4-6 (NIV)

I am gifted

"There are different kinds of gifts, but the same Spirit distributes them. There are different kinds of service, but the same Lord. There are different kinds of working, but in all of them and in everyone it is the same God at work." 1 Corinthians 12:4-6 (NIV)

Since I was young, I had always dreamed of being a teacher and a missionary. I always thought it was because of my family's legacy. Both of my grandmothers were in education and served as missionaries at one point. I figured it was in my blood. It was not until after college I got a glimpse into an even deeper calling on my life.

Have you ever taken the spiritual gifts quiz to see what your gifts are? I encourage you to take the quiz in the challenge section today. God made each one of us for a purpose, and for that purpose, He has equipped us with unique gifts from the Holy Spirit.

God gives us the gifts to accomplish what He calls us to do. I didn't take a spiritual gift test until after college. When I took it, a few missing puzzle pieces fell into place for me. I found out one of my gifts is apostleship, which is just a fancy way of saying I adjust to cultures easily. Hence, that desire to move to another country.

Another gift was faith and another giving. Since finding out about my gifts, I have been able to put them into practice. For one, I moved to Ghana. I have learned to give sacrificially and love it. And my faith has grown as God has stretched me in some crazy ways.

"Now you are the body of Christ, and each one of you is a part of it." 1 Corinthians 12:27 (NIV)

Spiritual gifts are also a way for us to help build the Church or our family of other believers. Just after Paul writes about the spiritual gifts (1 Corinthians 12:1-11), he talks about the body of Christ (1 Corinthians 12:12-30). As parts of the body of Christ, we all have a different role to play. And each role has different gifts to go with it. It is a beautiful picture of God's masterful plan to create us, equip us, and use us to bring His love into the dark world. You and I are a part of it. Let us intentionally find out our spiritual gifts He's chosen just for us and then use them for His glory.

Challenge: Take a spiritual gifts test online. One can be found here: https://spiritualgiftstest.com. Once you know your spiritual gifts, spend time asking God how He wants you to use them. May God equip you to shine a light in your corner of the world and bring love through divinely using your spiritual gifts.

Prayer: Thank You for giving me spiritual gifts, God. Please reveal to me what these gifts are and how I can begin using them even where I am now. Please embolden me to get out of my comfort zone to use my gifts, not being afraid of what others may think or how the outcome might be. Please help me to use these gifts for Your glory. I love You. Amen.

I am a creator

"O Lord, how manifold are Your works! In wisdom have You made them all; the earth is full of Your creatures."
Psalm 104:24

One of my favorite things to do is to create something out of nothing special. I can take a blank space, water, paint, and a brush and make a beautiful landscape. I can take sticks from someone else's trash and make a DIY house project. I can turn a room with ugly furniture into an oasis. But I could not have done any of that without my Father's DNA in me. And I cannot do anything as creative as He has done.

"In the beginning, God created the heavens and the earth."
Genesis 1:1

I have seen some pretty spectacular landscapes in my life. From the rolling, green hillside of Scotland, to the vast, deep Grand Canyon, to the dangerous yet glorious glaciers in Alaska—God is very creative, indeed. Not only do the varying landscapes show His creativity, but the diversity of the animals and birds and even the bugs. Did you know scientists have discovered 1.7 million different species of animals on our planet? [17] And that is only the ones people have found. One study says that 86 percent of the earth's species are yet to be discovered[18.] If we think of the uniqueness of the worm compared to the elephant and the swordfish, how can we not see how creative God is by looking at His creation?

All those creative juices are inside of you and me, too. We have been created in His image, meaning that we were made with some of the same attributes as He has. Creativity is one of those. Now, you may think you have no creative bone in your body. But I would challenge you to think outside the box. Creativity is not only the art projects moms hang on the fridge. Creativity can be shown in so many ways. Maybe you are a writer, a scientist, an actor, a musician, a cook, or a deep thinker. There are so many ways you can use your inerrant creativity to show God's majesty to the world.

Challenge: Do something creative. It can be something as small as doodling on this page to a big project like cooking your family dinner for the night. Praise God in your spirit as you use your creativity for the gift of recognizing and using creativity.

Prayer: Thank You for the creativity You have shown us in Your creation. Thank You for creating me in Your image and showing me I am also a creator. I give You my praise today as I create for Your glory. I love You. Amen.

I am an encourager

"Therefore encourage one another and build one another up, just as you are doing." 1 Thessalonians 5:11

Have you experienced someone encouraging you at just the right moment? Maybe you were having a bad day, and someone you didn't even really know gave you a word of encouragement. Or perhaps it was a teacher or boss praising your work? Or a friend telling you how much your friendship means to them?

I once felt low and unmotivated. Honestly, I was on the verge of quitting. Then I got this text from someone I barely knew at church. I could not even remember her name, to be honest. But her text lifted my spirits so much. She said, "God sees you. He cares about you. Don't give up." It was exactly what I needed to hear. A stranger, no less! She listened to the leading of the Holy Spirit, and He used her to encourage me that day.

Has that ever happened to you? Honestly, God has encouraged me more times than I can count. God is the great Encourager. He knows exactly what we need and will encourage us just the right way. Maybe it is a word of encouragement from a friend, a song on the radio at just the right time, or a sermon you needed to hear. The list goes on for ways God encourages His children.

"Blessed be the God and Father of our Lord Jesus Christ, the Father of mercies and God of all comfort, who comforts us in all our affliction, so that we may be able to comfort those who are in any affliction, with the comfort with which we ourselves are comforted by God." 2 Corinthians 1:3-4

Like Christ, He wants us to comfort and encourage others as He has comforted us when we need it. Who knows what word of encouragement you could bring someone today?

Challenge: Ask God to show you someone you can encourage right now. You could send a text or email or call them up. Speak what God puts on your heart to say. If nothing comes to mind, speak the truth over that person. They are loved; they are wanted; they are called beloved. Choose to be an encourager today.

Prayer: Lord, thank You for always encouraging me exactly when I need encouragement. Thank You for caring for me in that way. Please open my eyes to ways I can build up others today. Embolden my words and actions today so I am not afraid to be kind to others, even strangers. Please use my encouragement to boost someone else's spirit today. I love You. Amen.

I am a helpmate

*"An excellent wife who can find?
 She is far more precious than jewels.
The heart of her husband trusts in her,
 and he will have no lack of gain.
She does him good, and not harm,
 all the days of her life.
Strength and dignity are her clothing,
 and she laughs at the time to come.
She opens her mouth with wisdom,
 and the teaching of kindness is on her tongue.
She looks well to the ways of her household
 and does not eat the bread of idleness.
Her children rise up and call her blessed;
 her husband also, and he praises her:
'Many women have done excellently,
 but you surpass them all.'
Charm is deceitful, and beauty is vain,
 but a woman who fears the LORD is to be praised."*
Proverbs 31:10-12, 25-30

Women are special to God. When He looked at Adam, the first man, He saw he needed a helper, so He created a woman. Many women may twist this as a bad thing – I'm not just a helper to men, they may say. But I don't think that's what the point is here.

God created women for a special purpose. Men cannot do what we women were made to do (in more ways than one). And vice versa.

Nowadays, there is confusion about the definition of a woman, let alone who we were created to be. The world's definition of gender and sexuality is far away from what God intended for us. But when you go back to the beginning, back to the basics, you see that God created woman as a special gift to man and the world. We women are very special in God's plan, and our role is unique.

"Then the LORD God said, "It is not good for the man to be alone. I will make a helper who is just right for him."
Genesis 2:18

When God created the first woman, Eve, He did so to make a "helper" or a helpmate for Adam. There are many commentaries on what exactly the term helpmate means. It does not, in any way, mean inferior, servant, or non-leader[19]. Instead, the Hebrew word *ezer kenegdo*, means counterpart who saves—one who is separate, different, but equal, who is strong and rescues. Not only does this term represent woman, but throughout Scripture, authors use it to describe God, our ultimate Helpmate, Deliverer, and Savior.

Women are so important. We are the saviors who literally deliver nations through childbearing, and who can help build, create, lead, and drive our families, businesses, neighborhoods, and churches. This is how God created women to be. This is how God created you to be.

Challenge: Write a thank you letter to a woman in your life who has encouraged you lately. Maybe your mom, grandmother, pastor or pastor's wife, teacher, or friend. Thank her for her role in your life

Ashley Djokoto

and encourage her in love. Spend time praying for her and other women in your life – to experience God's love in new ways and to feel empowered as a woman in God's Kingdom.

Prayer: Thank You, God, for creating me to be a woman. Thank You for calling me helpmate – strong deliverer. Lead me in the people I should love, the situations I should influence, the places I should go – all for Your glory. Let me grow in confidence in who You have created me to be. Let me not be swayed by society's definition of women, but rather, hold onto and speak the truth in love. I love You. Amen.

I am a watch[woman]

"You know as well as I that the day of the Master's coming can't be posted on our calendars. He won't call ahead and make an appointment any more than a burglar would. About the time everybody's walking around complacently, congratulating each other—"We've sure got it made! Now we can take it easy!"— suddenly everything will fall apart. It's going to come as suddenly and inescapably as birth pangs to a pregnant woman. But friends, you're not in the dark, so how could you be taken off guard by any of this? You're sons of Light, daughters of Day. We live under wide open skies and know where we stand. So let's not sleepwalk through life like those others. Let's keep our eyes open and be smart. People sleep at night and get drunk at night. But not us! Since we're creatures of Day, let's act like it. Walk out into the daylight sober, dressed up in faith, love, and the hope of salvation." 1 Thessalonians 5:1-8 (MSG)

When Jesus went to pray before Judas came with the henchmen to arrest Him that dark night, He asked His disciples to keep watch and pray (Matthew 26:36). What did they do instead? They fell asleep (v. 40). Not just once, but twice, even after Jesus told them temptation was at their door. I cannot help but wonder – if Peter had been praying in the garden as his Master had been, would he have denied knowing Jesus three times just a few hours later? After all, "the spirit indeed is willing, but the flesh is weak" (v. 41).

In ancient Israel, a watchman was always posted at the top of the wall of defense to ensure that if an attack was upon them, he could warn the people in time to defend themselves properly. If a watchman fell asleep on duty, it could be catastrophic. He would lose his job, if not his life.

That metaphor can still be used for Christ-followers today. God entreated His servant Ezekiel to be a watchman for the people of Israel, entreating them to turn back to God and away from their wicket ways (Ezekiel 3:17-21). God still implores us to be His watch[women] – to watch out for ourselves and our fellow believers as we wait for Jesus to come again. In Thessalonians, Paul encourages believers not to fall asleep and keep watch, much like the watchmen of the olden days. It's far too easy to be lulled to sleep, though. Netflix bingeing, mindless scrolling through social media, and endless hours of video games. It is extremely easy to lose track of time, and before you know it, you have wasted two hours on something you meant to do for twenty minutes.

Distraction is one of the major ways the enemy gets us to lose focus on what truly matters in this life. I am not saying video games, Netflix, or social media are wrong. But we need to watch how much time we spend on our devices compared to how much time we spend seeking God's presence. I am just as guilty as the next person, but through the years, I've seen how imperative it is for believers to withstand the temptation of distractions and spend time with the Father instead.

"Preach the word; be ready in season and out of season; reprove, rebuke, and exhort, with complete patience and teaching."

2 Timothy 4:2

Without spending time with God daily, how can we live how He wants us to live? How can we be ready to reprove, rebuke, and exhort ourselves and our brothers and sisters? How can we be prepared to stand against the enemy's schemes to distract, steal, and kill? We have an enemy. And he is ready to attack us. But if we diligently spend time with the One who has defeated this enemy once and for all, we can stand and be victorious. And we can lead others in the same way.

Challenge: Our time and choices matter. Reflect on how you have spent your time this past week. How much have you spent on school or work? On your relationships with family and friends? On your device? In the Word of God and prayer? Make some honest reflections on what is consuming most of your time, and if it is not God, try to make some boundaries that would help you prioritize prayer and studying the Word. For example, you could spend time in your Bible when you first get up or right before bed. Or you could choose not to check your phone until you spend time praying. Little boundaries like these can build healthy habits that draw you nearer to God and help you grow in your faith.

Prayer: Thank You, Father, for saving me and giving me this chance to be a watch-woman. Forgive me for not prioritizing You always. Help me set boundaries so I can spend more time with You. Help me never justify the distractions I choose instead of You. Convict my heart, Jesus, when I put anything before You. Please help me also challenge others to seek You first. I love You. Amen.

Part XII

I am surrendered

"If any of you wants to be my follower, you must give up your own way, take up your cross daily, and follow me."

Luke 9:23 (NLT)

I am surrendered

"Humble yourselves, therefore, under the mighty hand of God so that at the proper time He may exalt you." 1 Peter 5:6

Surrendering is not a popular word, let alone an attitude to have. Think of the movies, books, shows, and news we read and watch. When is it ever popular or helpful to surrender? The world likes to tell us that the opposite is true: if we surrender, we are weak, and to win, we must fight until we pulverize the other side. We must take revenge and get that bully back twice as bad as he got us. We must send that text to hurt our friend how she hurt us. But God says something different.

When Jesus made Himself known as the Messiah, many people automatically thought He would fulfill the long-ago prophecies by leading an army to defeat the enemy ruling over them at the time, the Romans. They thought He would be their political leader and king who would rise up and overthrow their oppressors by destroying Rome's hold on Israel. But that's not exactly what God had planned for His Son.

Instead, Jesus came as the suffering servant (Isaiah 53:5). He "humbled Himself by becoming obedient to death, even death on a cross" (Philippians 2:8) – an instrument that was used for the most painful torturous death you could imagine. He did not come to defeat Roman rule; He came to die.

As you would expect, many did not support Him once they realized He would not meet their mistaken expectations. But that did not stop Jesus. Jesus had a mission, and He was going to fulfill it. Ironically, He did defeat the Israelites' most formidable enemy (sin), bringing freedom and victory to everyone. But He did it in a different way than they expected. Instead of more war and bloodshed of their enemies, He surrendered His life and willingly gave his blood for the offering that would satisfy all people's sins for all eternity.

"If any of you wants to be my follower, you must give up your own way, take up your cross daily, and follow me."
Luke 9:23 (NLT)

His surrender brought life for me and you. Now, He asks that we surrender in the same manner as He has shown us. He asks us to take up our cross of surrender and follow His lead. Surrendering our desires, wants, and needs is not easy or fun, but it brings life abundantly. I have surrendered more times than I can count, and there's something much better waiting for me on the other side each time. Better friends when I surrendered to God's plan, a better wedding when I surrendered to God's timetable, and a better attitude when I surrendered to God's way of living. My list goes on. Take it from me that though difficult, surrendering to God and His plans for our lives is the best decision you can make.

Ashley Djokoto

Challenge: Think about the parts in your life in which you have not surrendered to God – maybe a friendship you know is bad for you, or a habit of lying or cheating you've picked up, or the pornography or profane music you digest regularly. Let go and surrender these secret areas of your heart to God now.

Prayer: Jesus, You didn't have to die for me, but You chose to deliver me from death by surrendering to a torturous death. How can I ever thank You enough? Help me surrender now to You. Please show me how I have not surrendered. Lead me in the path of righteousness for Your sake. Help me make decisions that would honor You today. I love You. Amen.

I am a servant

"Who then is the faithful and wise servant, whom his master has set over his household, to give them their food at the proper time? Blessed is that servant whom his master will find so doing when he comes. Truly, I say to you, he will set him over all his possessions." Matthew 24:45-47

God's ways are opposite to what our world says is good. Our society says more wealth, more pleasures, more fun, and more fame make you happy. If you look closely into any celebrity's life who is all about "more," you will find that is not true, however. God says the opposite. He told us through His Son that the happiest ones are servants.

Nowadays, we have a bitter taste when we hear servant. But the definition I am referring to is someone who is completely submitted and surrendered, with no will of their own. A servant of Jesus has committed fully to following Him. Someone who does the will of her Father no matter the cost. Someone who would lose her life so she can find it in Him.

"Whoever loves [her] life loses it, and whoever hates [her] life in this world will keep it for eternal life. If anyone serves me, [she] must follow Me; and where I am, there will my servant be also. If

Ashley Djokoto

anyone serves me, the Father will honor [her]." John 12:25-26

This is not as scary as you probably think it is right now. It is not terrifying craziness to surrender to the One who created you, knows you, and loves you. He loves you unconditionally (Jeremiah 31:3). He is fighting for you (Deuteronomy 3:22). He is working *everything* out for your good (Romans 8:28). His will for you is not scary, but good – oh so good! Being His servant is the best thing because those who have counted the cost and have chosen to serve Him will be blessed with joy, peace, love, and every spiritual blessing they could never get on their own terms.

Challenge: What are you holding back from God? What are you afraid of giving up? Spend some time meditating and ask God to reveal those things to you. Pray and ask God to help you surrender and count the cost. I know it is a scary prayer, but trust me, it's one of the most important and worthwhile prayers you'll ever pray.

Prayer: Jesus, I surrender to You. I give you my life, my time, my future, everything. I want to count the cost for You. Please help me give up the things holding me back from fully following You. I trust You; help my unbelief. I love You. Amen.

I am humble

"Do nothing from selfish ambition or conceit, but in humility count others more significant than yourselves. Let each of you look not only to his own interests, but also to the interests of others. Have this mind among yourselves, which is yours in Christ Jesus, who, though he was in the form of God, did not count equality with God a thing to be grasped, but emptied himself, by taking the form of a servant,] being born in the likeness of men. And being found in human form, he humbled himself by becoming obedient to the point of death, even death on a cross."
Philippians 2:3-8

I feel like, in this day and age, we are pressured to know everything. With so many resources at our fingertips, it is much easier to find information and become an expert at just about anything. Why am I coughing? Why is he acting like that? What is the square root of 22? Google it. The internet is full of information, some true, some misleading, but information just the same.

One of my quirks is looking up my symptoms and diagnosing myself on Google or WebMD. My husband gets on to me when I do this; he says I should let the doctors do their job. I like to know and understand so I can hold the doctor accountable. But that's kind of ridiculous of me. I want to keep the doctors accountable.

Me, who doesn't have any medical background or degree, who's never studied medicine or anything related? The doctors are the ones who have trained and studied and should know the best medicine to use and the best treatments to give. Who am I?

But that is so like our culture. It is the way we have been trained. You have to know and understand everything. You have to be the boss, or you are a nobody. You have to be the smartest, or you have failed. You must be the prettiest and most popular, or you are nothing.

But that is not the way God has created us to be. We are not meant to know and understand everything, nor are we meant to be the best at everything. We are meant to be humble before man and before God.

"Clothe yourselves, all of you, with humility toward one another, for 'God opposes the proud but gives grace to the humble.' Humble yourselves, therefore, under the mighty hand of God so that at the proper time he may exalt you" 1 Peter 5:5-6

Just look at Jesus. He is the Boss. He is the King of Kings and Lord of Lords. Yet, He humbled Himself and became like us for the sole purpose of dying a painful death on the cross so we can live forever. He humbled Himself to that death for our sake. And He did not just humble Himself at His death, but also while He was alive on earth. He left heaven and glory to be made in all of man's futility so He could sleep on the ground and in tents, minister to the sick, poor, and unpopular people around Him, and face a lot of opposition and discrimination from the leaders at that time.

That took a lot of humility. And that is what He's asking of us as well. It won't necessarily look exactly like He did – sleeping on the streets and dying for our enemies – but it will be hard, nonetheless. Humility is intentionally putting others above ourselves. It is looking for ways to be kind and generous to others. It is acknowledging we don't know it all, and that's okay. It is putting our trust and hope in God and not in ourselves. That is the kind of humility Christ had and the kind of humility He wants for us.

Challenge: Choose one of the gospel books to read (Matthew, Mark, Luke, or John). Highlight how Jesus made Himself humble. Meditate on ways you could act like He did towards others. Spend time praying for opportunities to be humble.

Prayer: Thank You, Jesus, for leaving Your throne to save us. Thank You for showing us what humility looks like. Please help me to be humble. Let my actions, thoughts, and words be humble before You. As Your Word says, I trust that You will lift me up at the proper time. Help me trust You more. I love You. Amen.

I am kind

"Be kind to one another, tenderhearted, forgiving one another, as God in Christ forgave you." Ephesians 4:32

*B*eing kind is popular these days. But then again, a lot of society's messages focus on being kind to yourself, not others. With the mottos of "me first" and "love yourself" in many books and movies, it's not difficult to start to think those mottos make sense.

There is a story that Jesus told when a lawyer asked what it meant to be kind to one's neighbor: the story of the good Samaritan (Luke 10:25-37). The long and short of it is this: A Jewish man was attacked and left for dead. Two super-religious men passed him, thinking their endeavors were much more important than a near-dead man. An enemy of the Jewish people, however, chose to not only save his life but also provide and pay for his transportation, food, supplies, and hotel until he recovered.

When Jesus told this story, He meant for the lawyer to love and show kindness in the same way – even going out of his way to show kindness to strangers and enemies. A tough truth to swallow, not only for this lawyer at the time but for us as well. How can we show kindness to strangers or, worse, to those who hate us or mock us? God will give us the power if we choose to obey Him this way.

"Since you judge others for doing these things, why do you think you can avoid God's judgment when you do the same things? Don't you see how wonderfully kind, tolerant, and patient God is with you? Does this mean nothing to you? Can't you see that his kindness is intended to turn you from your sin?"
Romans 2:3-4 (NLT)

In the same way that God's kindness turns us from our sin, our kindness could be the catalyst that changes someone's heart of stone into a heart of flesh (Ezekiel 36:26). You never know what good could come out of leaving that one-hundred-dollar bill behind or giving up your Saturday morning to mow your neighbor's lawn, or even simply praying for that girl who spreads lies about you and your friends. So be brave, choose kindness, and God will do the rest.

Challenge: Think of some ways you could practically implement kindness this week. Pray over your ideas and ask God to help you to choose kindness this week.

Prayer: Thank You for Your kindness to me, Father. Thank You for leading me to repentance through Your kindness on the cross. Please open my eyes to opportunities to show kindness to others, even my enemies. Please give me boldness and faith when the opportunities present themselves. Let the kindness I show be a catalyst for change in someone else's life. Thank You for using me in this way. I love You. Amen.

I am content

"I know what it is to be in need, and I know what it is to have plenty. I have learned the secret of being content in any and every situation, whether well fed or hungry, whether living in plenty or in want. I can do all this through him who gives me strength."
Philippians 4:12-13 (NIV)

You may have heard Philippians 4:13 often – "I can do all things through Him who gives me strength." But have you read it within context? What is it referring to – all these things I can do? The verse before talks about the art of being content no matter what circumstances you find yourself in. I can be content because of this secret – God will help me by giving me the strength to be content.

I have to admit, I have never known true hunger. I have never been in a situation where I could not afford my next meal or did not have a roof over my head. Maybe you have. Paul did. He knew what it meant to have nothing to his name and to be homeless. He was even kicked out of town in not-so-nice ways several times. He also knew what it meant to have plenty. I find myself more in that boat, although I can talk myself into the idea that I don't have enough a little too quickly.

Before the verses about contentment, Paul wrote about how we can achieve contentment. It is all a matter of the mind. Philippians 4:8 lists the things we should think about – whatever is true, honorable, just, pure, lovely, commendable, excellent, worthy of praise – and omits what we should not think about – lack, anxiety, worry.

We don't have to worry about what we don't have. That is the art of being content in a nutshell. Trust God that He will supply everything we need in His perfect timing. Give your cares to Him because He cares for you. He is working on your behalf.

There have been several times when I did not know how I would purchase something I needed. One time, I was running low on money and was starting to worry about how I would fly home (to Ghana). I was visiting my parents and grandmother for the summer and had everything ready to go, but the COVID tests and last-minute travel expenses were starting to add up, and I didn't know if I had the money. I remember asking God to provide a specific amount of money to help me. A few hours later, my grandma called me into her room and gave me a check for – you guessed it – the exact amount of money I had asked God for. When I told her it was from God, we rejoiced. An hour later, she called me back in and gave me another check for the same amount, telling me the first one was from God and the second was from her.

I still chuckle inside when I think of that. Without meaning to, she double blessed me that day. I know it was God – because all good gifts come from above – who did not just provide the amount I asked for but doubled it. Our God will indeed "supply every need of [ours] according to His riches in glory in Christ Jesus" (Philippians 4:19). We do not need to be worried because He will provide. We can be content in whatever circumstances we may find ourselves in.

Challenge: Read Philippians 4 and turn it into a prayer for yourself.

Prayer: Lord, help me not to be anxious about anything, but rather give You all my worries and fears. Give me the peace of God, which I cannot even begin to understand. Help me think about what is true, noble, good, and pure. Help me to remember I can be content when I trust in You and choose not to worry. Help me put these things into action today. Amen.

Journal

Part XIII

I am a witness

"And they overcame and conquered him because of the blood of the Lamb and because of the word of their testimony, for they did not love their life and renounce their faith even when faced with death."

Revelations 12:11 (AMP)

I am a witness

"And they overcame and conquered him because of the blood of the Lamb and because of the word of their testimony, for they did not love their life and renounce their faith even when faced with death." Revelations 12:11 (AMP)

I really enjoy television shows about lawyers and court. It is fascinating to see how the intricacies of the law play out in court with "Objection!" and, "Nothing but the truth" ringing justice through the proceedings. Of course, I know that the actual court of law is not as glamorous or dramatized as the TV version.

In both courts – real and imagined – there are witnesses. No matter what court case you are dealing with – the supreme court or a misdemeanor court - both will need witnesses. People who can testify about the who, what, when, where, and why of the circumstances in question. People who will sway the jury or the judge in what to believe based on the testimony given. Witnesses are critical to how the trial turns out.

We are God's witnesses on this earth. When you accept Jesus as your Savior and start following Him, you become a witness for Him. Your job is now to testify – or tell everyone about who Jesus is, what He has done in your life, and why He loves us so much. We can do this by imitating Him in our daily actions.

"Therefore, be imitators of God, as beloved children."
Ephesians 5:1

Imitating Jesus is easier said than done, as I am sure you are aware. It is hard to love our enemies, put others first, and trust God no matter what. It is beyond difficult. But God will help us through; He will grow us and our faith until we realize we look so much more like Him than we did a year ago. One step, one day at a time, He will shape us to look, act, and sound more like Him. And that can be our greatest witness in the world.

Challenge: Confess anything that you are choosing to take a part of that is not in line with God's Word. These things can be a deterrent to our witness to others. If people question whether you are really a "Christian," it might be time to reexamine your life and your choices. That is not to say we'll never mess up as Christians, but if seasons change and you're still caught up in this sin or that sin, it is time to let go and let God transform you. Surrender to Him and actively choose to walk as an imitator of Him. (Getting an accountability partner may also help if there is an addiction or habit that you are having trouble with. There is no shame in seeking help.)

Prayer: Thank You, God, for making me Your witness. Most of the time, I don't feel worthy of this task. Thank You that I don't need to be a perfect Christian to be Your witness; rather, I can show that in my weaknesses, You are strong, and in my darkness, You are the Light. Thank You for your steadfast love and faithfulness. Please help me imitate You in all I do, think, and say today. I love You. Amen.

I am full of love

"So we have come to know and to believe the love that God has for us. God is love, and whoever abides in love abides in God, and God abides in him." 1 John 4:16

I kind of love Valentine's Day. I act like I don't care, but I have always loved getting cards and chocolates and special gifts from those I love – friends, parents, and now my husband. Valentine's Day is a day to celebrate love. Not just romantic love, but friendship love and agape love as well.

In actuality, we should celebrate agape love—God's love for us—every day. Agape love is the truest, purest, perfect kind of love. One that never fades, never fails, and never runs out. God loves us in this way. No matter how we mess up or how we cannot measure up, His love for us remains. After all, God is love and will always love us. It is who He is.

Our love for Him and others, though, is where we fall short – I feel like I fall short more often than naught. But with the Holy Spirit's help, I am slowly becoming more like Jesus. I look increasingly like Him every time I choose to love someone with agape love, the selfless and giving love that looks like God's love for us.

"Put on then, as God's chosen ones, holy and beloved, compassionate hearts, kindness, humility, meekness, and patience, bearing with one another and, if one has a complaint against another, forgiving each other; as the Lord has forgiven you, so you also must forgive. And above all these put on love, which binds everything together in perfect harmony." Colossians 3:12-14

One time in high school, I felt God nudging me to say hi to a new girl in my band class. I knew it was God speaking to me. I also could tell the new girl was shy and had no friends yet. But I was shy and insecure – and selfish. You see, I didn't want my friends to think I was "weird" for talking to the new girl with an eclectic style. I will never forget telling the Holy Spirit "no" and going about my business. I found out later that the girl was a missionary kid who had grown up in Africa, and I regretted my choice even more. At the time, I was not brave enough to show love to a stranger.

But God, in His grace and goodness, has brought me a long way since. I have learned that because of the Holy Spirit's power at work within me, I am full of the agape love of Christ. And that same power of the Holy Spirit enables me to put that love into action, no matter my fear or insecurity. And if you believe in Jesus and you have put your trust in Him, that same power is in you and available to you. You, my friend, are also full of agape love, ready to be poured out for others to see and glorify our God in heaven (Matthew 5:16). Don't worry about not being brave enough to say hi or smile at a stranger. Don't let offense keep you from forgiving your sister or brother. Don't let fear keep you from being kind in a way you know to be correct. Let the agape love inside of you pour out, and as you do, you will look more and more like Jesus.

Ashley Djokoto

"Let all that you do be done in love." 1 Corinthians 16:14

Challenge: Though it may not be Valentine's Day, make some cards for those in your life whom you love. Say thank you and tell them why you love them.

Prayer: Thank You, Lord, for the agape love You have given us. Thank You for always loving me, even though I don't deserve it. Open my eyes to see opportunities to love others, even strangers. Embolden and empower me, Holy Spirit, to be kind, forgive, and show love to everyone around me. Let it all be for Your glory so that others may know You more. I love You. Amen.

I am created to love

"We love because He first loved us. Whoever claims to love God yet hates a brother or sister is a liar. For whoever does not love their brother and sister, whom they have seen, cannot love God, whom they have not seen. And He has given us this command: Anyone who loves God must also love their brother and sister."
1 John 4:19-21 (NIV)

When my husband and I were still in the dating stage, I remember this one moment so clearly because it showed me how much God loved me. We were sitting on the side of the road by my apartment, and talking late into the night after our dinner. We had been dating for a while by then, and I knew what an upstanding, godly, fun, thoughtful guy he was. I remember he put his arm around me and said he loved me. That was the first time either of us had said the L-word. I remember thinking, "Who am I to get such a good guy?" And God put this thought in my mind: "I love you, Ashley. That's why I gave you him– to show My love for you."

There have been a few other times when I was struck with the thought that Jesus is the One loving me in that moment through something my husband does. I think that is what it's supposed to be like. We show His love to others through our actions and words.

Ashley Djokoto

"In the same way, let your light shine before others so that they may see your good works and give glory to your Father who is in heaven." Matthew 5:16

As Jesus' hands and feet to the world, it is our job to act, speak, and love like Him. When people see us, they should see Him. They should wonder why we are patient in line, why we never complain, or why we speak kindly about someone who hurt us. We should look different than the world because Jesus is different.

Challenge: Read 1 Corinthians 13:4-8 and list the adjectives used to describe love. Write one way you have shown this kind of love to someone in the recent past. For example, next to patient, you could write you didn't snap at your little brother who was annoying you. Or, next to not resentful, you could write how you forgave your friend for doing that unfair thing. Next to the adjectives you could not think of anything, brainstorm ways to better carry out that kind of love. Pray and ask God to give you opportunities to love others.

Prayer: Lord, thank You for the unconditional love in which You love me. Thank You for the countless ways You have shown me love through the people You have put in my life. Help me love them, too, as You have described in Your Word. I know I can show my love and gratitude for You by loving others this way. Please help me, for I cannot do it without Your help. I love You. Amen.

I am a gardener

"I planted, Apollos watered, but God was causing the growth. So then neither the one who plants nor the one who waters is anything, but God who causes the growth. Now he who plants, and he who waters are one; but each will receive his own reward according to his own labor." 1 Corinthians 3:6-8 (NASB)

I am very sad to say that I am not a green thumb. Most of the plants I've gotten have died within a month. I have killed even the cute succulent plants that are supposedly impossible to kill. I am a hopeless gardener.

Thankfully, that is not true when it comes to spiritual gardening which is a task that God has called all of us to do. One of the last things Jesus told his disciples before He ascended into heaven was to go out into the world and make disciples and teach them everything (see Matthew 28:19-20). Our job is to spread the good news to everyone, hoping they will receive God's love and be rescued from sin and death, too. I can tell you that it is not easy to follow through on this command. Especially in a world like ours.

But that is the amazing thing; Jesus did not just leave us on our own to follow through; He sent the Helper to help us and help others see and accept. It is impossible to do this without the Holy Spirit's help.

Ashley Djokoto

"...the Head, from whom the whole body, nourished and knit together through its joints and ligaments, grows with a growth that is from God." Colossians 2:19

When we love others, share our testimonies with them, and pray for them, we plant seeds of the knowledge of God in their minds and hearts. And that is all we do. Plant seeds. The Holy Spirit will do the rest. You and I cannot make someone grow spiritually, no matter how hard we try. Instead, let us do our part of planting seeds and let God do the rest.

Challenge: List three people you know who do not have a personal relationship with Christ. Spend time praying for them and asking God to provide ways for you to love them and speak about God to them.

Prayer: Thank You, Lord, for that You are the One who will cause growth – in my life and others' lives. Help me see opportunities You put in my way to love and serve others. Give me opportunities to speak about what You have done in my life. Please help me be bold enough to speak. Grow me, Lord. I love You. Amen.

I am an ambassador

"We are therefore Christ's ambassadors, as though God were making his appeal through us. We implore you on Christ's behalf: Be reconciled to God." 2 Corinthians 5:20 (NIV)

Growing up, I never really understood this verse about being God's ambassador too much. Sure, I have to share Jesus with others. But now, after living in a foreign country for nine years, I understand the necessity of ambassadors a bit more. Ambassadors are those who represent the nation from which they are from. For example, the American ambassador in Ghana represents America to Ghana. Not only that, but the role of the American ambassador is to cultivate positive, peaceful relationships with other nations, provide necessary resources and services for American citizens abroad, and even offer non-citizens a way to travel to America via the visa process. Ambassadors have a considerable role, don't they? Maybe that is why they get all the perks.

In the same way, you and I are ambassadors of Jesus. We are His representatives here on earth, showing others what He would sound like, act, and be like. That is a pretty tall responsibility in itself. We also have the role of cultivating peace in our schools, families, and other relationships, as well as guiding others in God's Word, and giving opportunities for outsiders to belong to our

Ashley Djokoto

family. This job is a lot and not at all easy to accomplish. Thankfully, God helps us to live and to act according to His purpose (Philippians 2:13). And like earthly ambassadors, we have some pretty great perks, too – eternal life (John 3:16), every spiritual blessing (Ephesians 1:3), and an inheritance that will never fade (Ephesians 1:14).

"Because we understand our fearful responsibility to the Lord, we work hard to persuade others. God knows we are sincere, and I hope you know this, too." 2 Corinthians 5:11 (NLT)

So, practically speaking, how can we be these ambassadors for Jesus who show others how amazing Jesus is and how great and wonderful it is to be a part of His family? It truly relies on how we represent Him in our daily lives. How do we act when we are with our friends? How do we speak to our parents? What do we write on social media? What do we pray for, and how much time do we spend with God? These are the cruxes of our lives. This is where it matters. Are you following Jesus' example, or are you following the crowd? Are you willing to do something uncool because it is right? Are you willing to go out of your way for others, though you would rather stay in your shell? If you are willing, God will work in you to be a witness for Him. He will meld you and form you to look more like Him in each action you take and each word you speak. All you have to do is say yes.

Challenge: Write down the name of one person you know who doesn't believe in Jesus. Spend time praying for that person. Then, write down some ways you can represent Jesus to them. Ask God for more ideas if you are stuck. Then, spend time praying for an opportunity to do one of the things on your list.

Prayer: Jesus, thank You for choosing and equipping me to be Your ambassador. I know I don't do a great job at it a lot of the time—please forgive me for not choosing to represent You in certain areas of my life. I surrender these to You now. Help me represent You well to those around me. Help me act like you and sound like You in all I do. Make me more like You. I love You. Amen.

Journal

Part XIV

I am created for relationships

> "And let us consider how to stir up one another to love and good works, not neglecting to meet together, as is the habit of some, but encouraging one another, and all the more as you see the Day drawing near."
>
> Hebrews 10:24-25

I am created for relationships

"And let us consider how to stir up one another to love and good works, not neglecting to meet together, as is the habit of some, but encouraging one another, and all the more as you see the Day drawing near." Hebrews 10:24-25

I have been super blessed to have amazing friends at every season of my life. From college, it can be hard to meet people, but God brought three wonderful friends, and we are still friends to this day, even though I moved across the ocean. Even here, in Ghana, God has provided a good community for me. Part of the expat life is saying goodbye to friends, but somehow, new friends have always come to replace the old. I know this is because God created us for friendships with others. We are not meant to live as islands.

When Jesus came – God incarnate and filled with the Holy Spirit – He did not stay off by Himself, though He could have. Instead, He chose twelve men to walk with Him everywhere He went. They ate together, traveled together, laughed together, served together. They did life together.

That is what God wants for you and me. That is what He intended the Church to be for us as believers. A people who love God and love each other – no matter what.

Do you have a community you belong to? A group where you can be yourself and where you know they will love you no matter what? Do you have people you can be honest with and tell your innermost desires to, knowing you can trust them? If so, cherish them. Grow those relationships even deeper. If not, I would encourage you to start praying for a community. Sometimes, churches, workplaces, or schools can be a good place to find it. Maybe you need to put yourself out there. I know it can be scary. My shy side can come out, and the last thing I want to do is make small talk. But it is so worth it when you take a step of faith to get to know someone, and you find a friend on the other side.

"A friend loveth at all times, and a brother is born for adversity."
Proverbs 17:17

Challenge: Pray for a life-giving community. If you feel like you already have a community like that, spend time thanking God and praying for those who have been there for you.

Prayer: Thank You, Jesus, that You lived Your life in the community to show us that community is essential. Please bring a life-giving community into my life. Please help me put others first so my relationships can grow. Please help me discern when I choose my friends. I want a community like You had. I love You. Amen.

I am a daughter

"But when the fullness of time had come, God sent forth His Son… to redeem those who were under the law, so that we might receive adoption as [daughters]… So you are no longer a slave, but a [daughter], and if a [daughter], then an heir through God."
Galatians 4:4-5, 7

Daddy's little girl. I don't know if that was fully me growing up, but I was lucky enough to have a dad who healthily portrayed God to me. My dad was my provider. He was my protector. When I was afraid, I would go into my parents' bedroom and sleep on their floor. I knew my dad would protect me from the bad guys. As I grew older, my dad was my cheerleader. He urged me to do my best and showed compassion when I failed. He helped me in many ways, more than I probably even realize: with my car that broke down almost every weekend, my glitchy computer, and my homework – He even helped me build a wooden flute and do a whole science project on whether the pitch is affected by temperature. My dad showed me what a good marriage looks like, too. He and my mom have faithfully married for over 30 years, which is a reason for celebration nowadays.

I know not all earthly dads measure up, but our earthly fathers are just a glimpse of who our heavenly Father is. Where our earthly fathers fall short, our heavenly Father never will. He is our ultimate provider, protector, cheerleader, and helper. He will always come through for us, period.

There is a special bond between dads and daughters, though. Just look at the movies and books out there. There is something special about a dad who loves his daughters and will do anything for them. Just as a dad adores his daughters, God the Father adores us, His daughters. He loves us. He even died for us so we could have a relationship with Him. He will never abandon His daughters. He will always fight for us. He will love us forever and ever.

And as His daughters, we have special perks. We are His heirs. An heir possesses the rights to all the inheritance from the father. In essence, God has given us the right to steward everything in creation. He is now expecting us to treat His creation as He does, with love and care. As His daughters, we are called to be like our Father in stewarding the things He has given us and showing His steadfast love to others.

Challenge: Read Ephesians 1:1-14 and note what it says about our inheritance. Reflect upon all that God your Father has done for you. How has He been your protector, provider, and encourager? Thank Him for His steadfast love and the inheritance He has given us through His Son.

Prayer: Thank You, Father! You not only redeemed me as your daughter, but You have given me an inheritance that will not perish or disappear. You are a good, good Father. Thank you for being my protector, provider, and biggest encourager. Thank you for all that You have given me. Please help me to be a good daughter and share this amazing love with others today. I love You. Amen.

I am a sister

*"For all who are led by the Spirit of God are children of God…
Now if we are children, then we are heirs – heirs of God and co-heirs with Christ" Romans 8:14, 17 (NIV)*

My sisters are some of my favorite people in the world. I've been blessed to have three sisters – one older and two younger. I count them among my closest friends. Though we don't always agree and have different personalities and perspectives, they are my sisters, and I love them. We have gotten into plenty of fights through the years. Once, I was so mad at one of my sisters that I cut her finger with scissors! In retaliation, she shut the car window on my head. But despite the many fights and disagreements, we love each other. We are family.

"For whoever does the will of God, he is my brother and sister and mother." Mark 3:35

Amazingly, Jesus calls us His sisters. We are His family. When we mess up, it is okay because our brother Jesus has made a way for us. He has got our back. Something I always wanted growing up was a big brother. Someone who would look out for my good in school as I made my way in the world, someone who would make sure no one picked on me and showed me the best way to get things done. I guess I've always had that in Jesus. He has protected me, though I don't always realize it. He has made a way for me to make my place in the world, and He has shown me the best way to do things through His Word. When I'm down, He lifts me and encourages me. Just like I imagine a big brother would do, except I don't get in fights with Jesus.

He is our big Brother, our Shield, our Protector against the bullies of the world, the One who gives us the best advice. He is better than any earthly sibling because He won't mess up. He will always have our back. He knows all things and works everything out for the best (Romans 8:28). And because we have Jesus in our lives, we can be good sisters to others. Did you know even if you are technically an only child, you have millions of brothers and sisters around the world? When Scripture tells us we are in God's family, it means we are sisters to all of His children. That is amazing to me. And as sisters, we can love, encourage, and pray for our brothers and sisters in need.

Challenge: Look up the World Watch List for the countries with the most persecution from Open Doors. Spend time reading about the countries on the list and praying for our brothers and sisters in those countries.

Prayer: Jesus, thank You for being my Chief Protector and Guide. Thank You for accepting me into Your family as Your sister. Thank You for giving me millions of other brothers and sisters worldwide. Help me remember to pray for them today, especially those facing persecution. May your grace abound to them today. I love You. Amen.

I am a friend

"What is man that you are mindful of him, and the son of man that you care for him?" Psalm 8:4

Do you have a friend that is more like a sister? Someone you could be with all day, and you would not get tired of each other's company? Someone who you can be yourself with? Someone who will call you out on your stuff?

I have been lucky enough to have such a friend in almost every season of my life. I did go through a stage in high school, though, where it felt like no one understood me. I felt like I was alone. I had friends, but I didn't feel like myself around them. I constantly tried to "fit in" and be "well-liked" by everyone. It was exhausting. But it ended up being a good thing – my loneliness. Because I felt like no person could understand me, I grew closer to Jesus. He became my best friend. I told Him everything. I learned to pray. I learned to trust Him. I learned to love myself. It was not an easy process, but through His friendship with me, I learned what it means to be His friend.

"Greater love has no one than this, that someone lay down his life for his friends. You are my friends if you do what I command you. No longer do I call you servants, for the servant does not know what his master is doing; but I have called you friends, for all that I have heard from my Father I have made known to you." John 15:13-15

In John 15, Jesus says these profound words: "You are my friends." Wow, pause for a minute and think about that. You are Jesus' friend. This Jesus, who is GOD incarnate, is YOUR friend. He is someone you can tell your deepest secrets, fears, and longings to, and you know He won't laugh or tell others. He will always treat you with love and respect and never turn His back on you or betray you. He is always there to talk to, even in the middle of the night. He is your forever friend.

He is the kind of friend I always want in my corner. And the best part? He cannot have too many friends! And He will be the same reliable friend that He has been to me to you, too. Because that is the kind of God He is.

Challenge: Try to be a better friend back to Jesus. Spend *more* time with Him. Talk to Him *more*. Set a goal for yourself today.

Prayer: Dear Jesus, thank you for being my friend. Thank you for being mindful of me and hearing me whenever I call. Thank You for always being there for me, no matter what. Help me prioritize our relationship this week. I love You. Amen.

I am a bridge

"For He Himself is our peace, who has made us both one and has broken down in His flesh the dividing wall of hostility by abolishing the law of commandments expressed in ordinances, that He might create in Himself one new man in place of the two, so making peace, and might reconcile us both to God in one body through the cross, thereby killing the hostility.." Ephesians 2:14-16

The world would have us believe we should be divided against each other, group by group. Social media shows us an *us versus them* way to live. If you and I disagree then we cannot be friends; in fact, we are enemies if we believe different things. But that should not be the case, friends. God created us to be bridge builders, not barricade builders.

Jesus is our Bridge. Jesus "broke down the barrier of the dividing wall... so that in Himself He might [establish] peace and reconcile [us] to God through the cross" (Ephesians 2:15-16). What was that wall? The wall was sin and death, hatred and bigotry, disobedience and apathy. He destroyed the barrier and became the Bridge connecting us back to light, truth, and love – to Himself. That should be our goal as His followers. We should want to build bridges between us and them.

"There is neither Jew nor Greek, there is neither slave nor free, there is no male and female, for you are all one in Christ Jesus."
Galatians 3:28

We are all equal in God's eyes. One day, we will all be together – people from every tongue, every tribe, and every nation will be in God's everlasting kingdom (Revelation 7:9). There will be no us and them, only us. It will be all inclusive, all equal, all praising God as one voice, one people. How amazing will that be? The thing is, we don't have to wait for heaven to experience such a thing. We cannot. God wants us to be bridge builders now, here. He wants us to go out of our comfort zone to befriend people who are different than us, even those we disagree with. It may be that you choose not to post that divisive post. Or it may be choosing to sit with that one girl at lunch. Or it may be praying for your enemies. How can you be a bridge builder in your corner of the world?

Challenge: Write down your groups of people – your family, friends, neighbors, classmates, etc. Then, think of some people you know who are outside of your groups. The outliers. The people who are so different from you that you don't ever think about them. How could you be a bridge builder for them? Could you reach out to them? Could you do something nice for them? Make a list of ideas and pray over them. Plan to do one of the things you listed this week.

Prayer: Lord, thank You for being *the* Bridge for me – for making a way to reconcile me to God. Please help me to be a bridge for others now. Show me the people You have placed in my life who may feel like outsiders. Help me show kindness to them and go out of my way to build a relationship with them, knowing they ultimately need You in their lives. I surrender to You. I love You. Amen.

Part XV

I am the Church

"Instead, we will speak the truth in love, growing in every way more and more like Christ, who is the head of His body, the Church. He makes the whole body fit together perfectly. As each part does its own special work, it helps the other parts grow, so that the whole body is healthy and growing and full of love."

Ephesians 4:15-16 (NLT)

I am the Church

"Instead, we will speak the truth in love, growing in every way more and more like Christ, who is the head of His body, the Church. He makes the whole body fit together perfectly. As each part does its own special work, it helps the other parts grow, so that the whole body is healthy and growing and full of love."
Ephesians 4:15-16 (NLT)

Throughout my life, I have attended many different churches: Baptist, nondenominational, Presbyterian, Orthodox, Pentecostal, and Catholic. Some were big; some were small. Some loud, some quiet. Some were welcoming, and others not so much. I have had some great, moving experiences in a church, and I have experienced loneliness and hurt inside a church. I have met some amazing people and some people who have ended up disappointing me. I have learned through the years that churches are made up of many messed up, broken people in need of grace. Can I get an amen?

When Jesus chose His first church leader, He didn't choose someone with a perfect rap sheet. He chose Peter, the one who had denied Him more than once and forsaken everything they had been building up for the past three years of ministry. From the outside, Peter looked like a big, fat failure. He had royally messed up. But Jesus looked past all that and chose him anyway.

"And I tell you, you are Peter, and on this rock I will build my church, and the gates of hell shall not prevail against it."
Matthew 16:18

God had chosen Peter from before time began to build His church after Jesus ascended back to the Father. He picked him, though He knew Peter would fail in his mission the first time, even reject knowing God the Son. God chose him all the same. And He has chosen you and me as well. Despite our failings and mess-ups, God chose us from before time to be a part of His family as the institution we now call Church. It is global. It is wide-reaching. It is accepting to all, no matter our failings. God's family, unified under Him, sent forth with one mind and the same mission.

Are we all perfect within this Church? Definitely not. But we are called to love and forgive as we have been forgiven (Ephesians 4:32). We are called to use our spiritual gifts and talents to serve our brothers and sisters in Christ (Ephesians 4:16). We are called to love unconditionally (1 Corinthians 13:7-8).

And when we accept this calling, it becomes the most beautiful thing. People from all races, all ethnicities, all professions, all ages— coming together, being unified, showing love and compassion, proclaiming truth. It is a beautiful picture. And while churches we attend often fall short of this picture, it still is our goal. And one day, it will be fulfilled when Jesus returns. Oh, how I cannot wait for that day.

Challenge: Read Ephesians 4 and write down all the ways we are called to love our brothers and sisters in Christ. Look over the list and see if there are any that are especially challenging for you.

Ashley Djokoto

Spend time praying over those things and think about ways to implement them in your life.

Prayer: Thank You, Jesus, for making a way for me to belong to your family. It is such a wonderful thing; I'm very grateful. Thank You for giving us special instructions on how to treat our brothers and sisters in the Church. Help me live up to these standards. Give me ideas today, Holy Spirit, on how I can better love those You have placed in my life. I love You. Amen.

I am the Bride

"For as a young man marries a young woman, so shall your sons marry you, and as the bridegroom rejoices over the bride, so shall your God rejoice over you." Isaiah 62:5

Marriage was created to be a picture of how much Jesus loves us, His Church, His Bride. The union between husband and wife is a metaphor for Christ's love and devotion to those who follow Him.

My husband and I got married during the Covid-19 pandemic. Needless to say, our plans were messed up more than a few times. We had planned for my family to come to Ghana, but even after postponing twice, the borders remained closed to visitors. It was not anything like I had imagined growing up or even planned when we got engaged, but it was everything we had prayed for. It was simple, and people heard the gospel of Jesus' love for us. My husband showed his happiness and thankfulness that day by dancing like he had never danced before. Even his mother was surprised. He is usually very reserved and quiet, but that day, after waiting for his bride (me!), he rejoiced by dancing to the Lord.

ASHLEY DJOKOTO

"For your Maker is your husband, the Lord of hosts is His name; and the Holy One of Israel is your Redeemer, the God of the whole earth He is called." Isaiah 54:5

That is what Jesus does. He rejoices over us with dancing and loud singing. We make Him that happy. We are His Bride. And one day soon, Jesus will return to this earth and call His Bride home. What a beautiful picture of true and perfect love. Marriage on this earth points us to the perfect union between Christ and His Church (us believers). It is a perfect partnership, with Jesus loving His Bride and His followers respecting, trusting, and surrendering to Him. (This picture is better painted in Ephesians 5:22-33.)

To those who long for a husband one day, keep praying and trusting that God has someone He has prepared for you. God will answer your prayers in His good timing. And while we are waiting, let us grow our relationship with our King, who will one day return and bring us to our forever home.

Challenge: Reflect on Zephaniah 3:17. Close your eyes and imagine your heavenly Father rejoicing and singing over you in gladness. Because He is. Spend time thanking God for all His goodness to you.

Prayer: God, I thank You for Your goodness to me! Thank You for the steadfast love and mercy You show me every day. Great is Your faithfulness. Thank You for choosing me and calling me Bride. Thank You that one day, You will return for us and deliver us once and for all. I love You. Amen.

I am the Body

"Now you are the body of Christ and individually members of it."
1 Corinthians 12:27

Have you ever experienced an injury that debilitates you from functioning normally? Maybe it was a migraine that kept you in bed or a broken bone that kept you from walking. Interestingly, your big toe has only two bones out of the 206 bones in your body, but if you break one, it can be excruciating to walk or even stand[20]. Who knew that your toe had that much importance?

Just as each of our body parts plays a vital role in our body, so do each of us play an essential role in the Church. The Bible equates the Church as Christ's Body. We are the hands and feet of Jesus. We are also the toes and ears and fingers and tongue. That may sound weird, but it is a metaphor for the vital role each of us has to play in this world.

"But as it is, God arranged the members in the body, each one of them as He chose. If all were a single member, where would the body be? As it is, there are many parts, yet one body." 1 Corinthians 12:18-20

Ashley Djokoto

Together, as one Body in Christ, as one Church, we can change the world. Just as when our bodies are working well together, so too, when we work together well, we can get a lot more accomplished.

It is like when you are given a group assignment. You could do the whole thing by yourself, but that would take more time and effort than if you were to divide the work between the group members, right? Who wants to spend four hours doing a project that could take only 30 minutes if delegated properly?

Now, some of you probably think that the outcome quality might be better if you alone take charge and do it yourself, depending on who your partners are. Tell me if you have not been there. I sure have, and I have chosen to do it myself because I know I would do a much better job. But that is kind of arrogant of us, isn't it? If we applied it to the Church, could we say we are any better than others? We have all fallen short of God's standard (Romans 3:23). No one can say they are better off than another; it is all by God's grace that we are where we are.

If we have the right attitude and perspective about what we deserve versus what we have gotten, we will be in a better mind to let others help us meet the unique assignment God has given us. And we will need a lot of help. God did not design us to work alone. We need each other. And so, we must humble ourselves and accept the other members of God's family, as well as their help.

Challenge: Call or text someone from your church or school you have not talked to in a while. Say an encouraging word or tell them you are praying for them. You would be surprised how much one "hello" can mean to someone.

Prayer: God, thank You for making me a part of something bigger than myself. Help me see myself correctly so I can love others well. Give me ideas to serve my brothers and sisters in Christ. Help my attitude never get in the way of loving and serving those around me. I love You. Amen.

I am beloved

"To all who are beloved of God in Rome, called as saints: Grace to you and peace from God our Father and the Lord Jesus Christ."
Romans 1:7 (NASB)

"You are God's beloved on your worst day, in your worst moment."[21]

Read that again. Doesn't that seem backward? How can God still love me as His beloved when I mess up and am at my absolute worst?

When I was a child, I had an anger problem. When I got angry, I literally saw red and could not help myself from reacting in some pretty unhealthy ways. It took the power of God's Word and prayer to get me out of that unhealthy habit. Now, people are surprised when I tell them this testimony because I have such a calm demeanor. I can only say it is because of God's grace and work in my life. But looking back, those were probably some of my worst moments – when I lost control and acted poorly. Yet, God whispered my name, called me His beloved, and helped me learn the art of letting go.

The same is true for you. Even at your worst moments, you are God's beloved. So much so that He sent Jesus to die for you and take away those worst sins forever, never to even think about them again (Isaiah 43:25).

"But now, O Jacob, listen to the LORD who created you. O Israel, the one who formed you says, 'Do not be afraid, for I have ransomed you. I have called you by name; you are mine.'" Isaiah 43:1 (NLT)

God knows your name. He knows the number of hairs on your head. He knows your every thought, wish, dream, and desire. He knows when you sleep and when you rise. He knows every intimate detail about you. And He still loves you. He still chooses you. He adores you. You are His Beloved. Isn't that amazing? The God of the Universe calls us by name. He created us, formed us in our mother's womb, and says we are His Beloved.

Challenge: Now, as we are His beloved, He wants us to show others His loving kindness and compassion by treating them as His beloved, too. Is there someone who you have a hard time loving or even liking? Write down their name and say a prayer for them because they are God's beloved, too. Spend time thanking God for His forgiveness and compassion towards us.

Prayer: Thank You, Jesus, for calling me beloved even at my worst moments. Thank You for Your loving-kindness and compassion towards us. Help me see others as You see them, Your beloved. I love You. Amen.

I am united

"There is one body and one Spirit —just as you were called to one hope when you were called — one Lord, one faith, one baptism; one God and Father of all, who is over all and through all and in all." Ephesians 4:4-6 (NIV)

Have you ever been to a sports game? Getting dressed up in your team colors, waving your flag proudly, getting swept up in the competition, and yelling, "Go team, go" with the rest of the crowd? Whether it is a small high school basketball team or a large stadium at a football game, something draws you in when you're a part of a crowd rooting for one team to win.

That is kind of what it's like for Christians. We are one team, rooting for one end goal - For all to know Jesus and follow Him. We are united in that goal, that vision as Christian brothers and sisters. We are family, and not only with the Christians you know of in your circle around you but with those who are spread wide and far in nations around the world. We are united with each other in Christ.

Now, I am not naive to think Christians always act like one big, united, happy family. Being a Christian can be hard. God has called us to be humble, meek servants who show loving-kindness to others, though they betray, slander, or even threaten us. Yet, somehow, when we choose to put others first in such a way, we are united further with our brothers and sisters worldwide.

"For you are all children of God through faith in Christ Jesus. And all who have been united with Christ in baptism have put on Christ, like putting on new clothes. There is no longer Jew or Gentile, slave or free, male and female. For you are all one in Christ Jesus." Galatians 3:26-28 (NLT)

There are countless stories throughout history when Christians have stepped up and have come together to bring hope and restoration after a devastating event. After the earthquakes in Turkey in 2023, when over fifty thousand people lost their lives, Christians rose up to help those in need[22]. In Mississippi, after a devastating tornado ripped across the state, leaving thousands homeless, Christians from all different denominations stepped up and donated time, money, and effort to see their state rebuilt despite the historical racial tensions in the area[23]. In my own life, when I have gone through my most difficult moments, my brothers and sisters in Christ have loved, encouraged, and pointed me back to God's truth.

Together, we are better. United, we will stand. These are not new ideas. And as the Church - God's people - with the help of the Holy Spirit, we have such opportunities to show this broken, divided world what it can look like when we put our differences aside to love each other. Because that is what Jesus did when He died for you, me, and all the nations and generations in this world (John 3:16). He died to bring us together as one. So, let us be challenged to do that today. Instead of focusing on our differences in theology, culture, background, or goals, let us focus on the fact that God has created and called each of us to be a part of His

Ashley Djokoto

family. And that is no small thing.

Challenge: Ephesians 4:2 tells us to bear with others in love. To bear with others in love means to show grace even when they don't deserve your grace because that is what Jesus does for us. Is there a fellow Christian who you have been holding a grudge against? Is there a brother or sister for whom you've harbored bitterness and unforgiveness? Talk to God about that person and try praying for them. Repent of any bitterness or unforgiveness and ask God to help you bear with those people in love.

Prayer: Jesus, thank You so much for making me a part of this vast family of other believers. Forgive me for when I have let unforgiveness, judgment, or bitterness deter me from loving my brothers and sisters in Christ as I should. Please help me work through these feelings and thoughts and bring me closer to you and others. Let your Church bring glory to Your Name when we show the world love and unity. Thank You for this opportunity. I love You. Amen.

Part XVI

I am Blessed

"The Lord bless you and keep you, the Lord make His face shine upon you, and be gracious to you, the Lord lift up His countenance upon you, and give you peace."

Numbers 6:24-26

I am blessed

"Blessed are the poor in spirit, for theirs is the kingdom of heaven. Blessed are those who mourn, for they shall be comforted. Blessed are the meek, for they shall inherit the earth. Blessed are those who hunger and thirst for righteousness, for they shall be satisfied. Blessed are the merciful, for they shall receive mercy. Blessed are the pure in heart, for they shall see God. Blessed are the peacemakers, for they shall be called sons of God." Matthew 5:3-9

To be blessed means to be endowed. In Matthew 5, Jesus used the term blessed to pronounce the good things we would receive if we followed Him. Not only followed Him but lay down our own self-pleasing goals to act and be more like Jesus. Blessed are the poor in spirit (knowing you have nothing of worth without Christ). Blessed are those who mourn. Blessed are the meek (humble and self-sacrificing). Blessed are those who hunger and thirst for righteousness (living rightly before God). Blessed are the merciful and pure in heart and peacemakers.

None of these sound all that appealing when you are busy trying to be "blessed" by the world's standards. Our prayer list often matches the mindset of keeping up with the Kardashians – more money, more friends, more clothes, more accolades, or more stuff. Not that any of those are bad things, but none of them are listed in

Jesus' definition of being blessed.

"Blessed rather are those who hear the word of God and keep it!"
Luke 11:28

Each promise given to those who decide to live as Jesus prescribes is focused on spiritual blessings – belonging to the kingdom of heaven, being satisfied in righteousness, receiving mercy. This shows us that the greatest blessing we could ever receive is more of God in our lives. I will leave you with one of the most beautiful passages in Scripture. This prayer was often spoken over the people of God as a blessing, a reminder of the One True God who was always with them and for them. May it be such a reminder to us as well.

"The Lord bless you and keep you, the Lord make His face shine upon you, and be gracious to you, the Lord lift up His countenance upon you, and give you peace." Numbers 6:24-26

Challenge: Watch Spoken Gospel's video on Matthew 5-7. Read all of Jesus' sermon (Matthew 5-7) and pay special attention to what the Holy Spirit may be leading you to repent of or obey. Spend time praying for God to equip and guide you to live like Jesus. Pray also for more blessings, especially more of Him in your life.

Prayer: Jesus, thank You for giving that sermon so many years ago. Please help me digest and obey all that You have said. Please help me become more like You so I can fully see the many blessings You have already given me. Let me not compare myself to others but rather be thankful for what I already have. Help me live a life that would glorify Your name. I love You. Amen.

I am highly favored

"For the Lord God is a sun and shield, the Lord bestows favor and honor. No good thing does He withhold from those who walk uprightly." Psalm 84:11

Mary was just a typical teenager living life, trying to follow God. She had her weaknesses and insecurities, just like the rest of us. She might have had a crush on Joseph, or she might have been scared to death of being married. She had friends and a family whom she loved but might have gotten on her nerves more than a time or two. She was an average teenager who loved God and tried her best to follow His ways.

And then, her life was completely interrupted. An angel visited her and told her that her entire world was about to change. She would be the mother of the Son of God. Her betrothed (fiancé) would be His father, though they were not technically married yet. And yet, the angel told her she was highly favored, for the Lord was with her.

"The angel went to her and said, "Greetings, you who are highly favored! The Lord is with you." Luke 1:28 (NIV)

You might be thinking, how does a world turned upside down reflect someone who is highly favored? Mary went on to live a very full life. She was one of the first to meet the long-awaited Messiah. Not only that, but He called her mother and loved her from the beginning. What a beautiful, rich life.

No matter our circumstances, we are highly favored in God's sight. The Lord is with us, and we are favored in His sight. Do you realize that we can do nothing apart from God (John 15:5)? Everything we are and everything we have is because He has given it to us. Every opportunity we have gotten and every possession we have is from Him. Every person we love and every gift we have been given is from Him. All of it is from God. We are *highly* favored. So, praise and thank Him for everything He has given you today.

Challenge: Make a list of things you are thankful for. You are highly favored. Thank God for the many things He has shown you favor for.

Prayer: Thank You, Lord, for calling me highly favored. Who am I that I would be counted among Your favored? And yet, You have blessed me with so much. Thank You! Let me always praise Your Name for the goodness You have bestowed upon me. I love You. Amen.

I am the head

"The Lord will make you the head, not the tail." Deuteronomy 28:13 (NIV)

Power. Glory. Fame. Success. Popularity. The most likes on TikTok. Our society points to all these things as points of success. If I had this much money, I would be happy. If I had a husband, I would be satisfied. If I were top of my class, I would be happy. The world pressures us to fit into the status quo box of what makes a person happy and on top of the world, but God's way is different.

When Jesus came to earth, He was coming as the King of Kings and Lord of Lords—the Ultimate Power in the entire universe. And yet, He did not come as a powerful, grown man but as a vulnerable, tiny baby. If you have ever interacted with newborns, they cannot do anything alone. Babies depend entirely on others to give them everything– food, cleanliness, safety, protection. That is how Jesus, this Most Glorious and Powerful King, came to our world.

I don't know about you, but if I were Jesus, I would have probably wanted to come to a nice mansion with everything catered to me. It is a good thing I am not Jesus because He came in this way to show us that His version of success and happiness looks a lot different than ours.

"So the last will be first, and the first last." Matthew 20:16

Jesus was in the business of making His upside-down kingdom known. Jesus lived a life that was backward from society. He was born into a low-income family; He was raised as a carpenter, which was a low-status job back in the day; His first visitors were shepherds, which was an even lower-status job; He spent His whole life serving others and obeying God's timetable. Jesus told His disciples this kind of life would make them the most happy and successful in this new kingdom. Being last would put you first in the new kingdom order and vice versa. To be the head, you must be a servant (Matthew 20:26). That is not popular even today.

But for those who have committed to following Jesus and His ways, it is the best news in the world. Even though people may reject us for our faith, laugh at us, mock us, or even physically harm us, God promises that we will have a place with Jesus in glory (2 Corinthians 5:1). This life is not the end of the story. If we follow the way of Servant Jesus, He will exalt us in due time (1 Peter 5:6). So be encouraged, sister; this is not the end.

Challenge: Think of someone you can serve today. You could write someone an encouraging note or text. You could babysit your younger siblings. You could clean up your neighbor's yard. Try to think of something that may put you out of your comfort zone and then do it. Every time you choose to serve others, it gets easier the next time. It is like a muscle in our brain that we must rewire to think of others above ourselves naturally. The only way to rewire it

Ashley Djokoto

is through practicing the art of serving others.

Prayer: Lord, thank You for shaking up this world when You came to live here. Thank You for making a way for us to be genuinely happy and content – not by gaining more of what this world offers, but by knowing You and serving others. Though it doesn't seem like it's always worth it to put others above myself, I pray that You would transform my heart to seek the good of others above myself. Help me to be a servant leader like You are. I love You. Amen.

I am confident

"Though an army encamp against me, my heart shall not fear; though war arise against me, yet I will be confident." Psalm 27:3

I think I have mentioned this before, but I was extremely shy when I was younger. I was never one to participate in class, and when my teachers called on me, I probably stuttered out a barely audible answer. It was not until college that I began to rid myself of the "shy" label I had attached to myself for so long. I began to pray that God would help me escape the pit of shyness I had inadvertently fallen (or dug) myself into, and slowly but surely, He did pull me out. Now, I am confident in who I am – in who God has created me to be. It took a lot of years and pain and struggle to get me to this side of confidence, though.

Maybe you have a similar story – You are not quite sure why God made you this way and struggle to feel the confidence you yearn to feel. Perhaps you are the opposite. You radiate confidence in such a way that spreads to others. Or maybe you are somewhere in the middle – Sure, you act confident on social media and to your friends, but inside, you question yourself almost constantly. Wherever you find yourself on the confidence journey, know you are not alone. Research shows that young women tend to struggle with low self-esteem more than young men, and this low self-esteem can lead to other health disorders such as depression, anxiety, and eating disorders[24]. But sister, let me stress that you are not alone. Knowing that most women your age struggle with the same things may help, but what will help even more is knowing Your Father in heaven looks down in love on you and wants you to come to Him about everything.

"Let us then with confidence draw near to the throne of grace, that we receive mercy and find grace to help in time of need."
Hebrews 4:16

We can have the confidence to draw near to God. We do not need to have fear, self-deprecation, or pity. Instead, we can have confidence. Confidence that God is who He said He is and that we are who God made us to be, failures and all. God knows we cannot do this life solo, so He made way for us to call on His name confidently. Through Jesus, we have 24-7 access to Him. And we can come to Him confidently, knowing that He alone is what we need to have more confidence in this turbulent and often challenging life.

Challenge: Review the list of I AM statements in the table of contents. These are all statements that define who you are in Christ. Which ones can you internalize today that will help grow your confidence in who God has created you to be? Spend time praying for more confidence in those areas.

Prayer: Thank You, Lord, for making me this way. Though I struggle to like myself some days, please remind me that You made me this way for a perfect reason, and there is no mistake in how I was made. Please grow my confidence in who I am in You, oh Lord. Thank you for opening a way for me to draw near to you confidently. I love You. Amen.

I am valued

"Since you are precious and honored in my sight because I love you, I will give people in exchange for you, nations in exchange for your life." Isaiah 43:4 (NIV)

Did you know the Bible says, "do not fear" 365 times? I think that's God's way of saying it's an important lesson to learn. It is in our human nature to worry and fear, however, so it is not an easy thing to do. During Jesus' ministry here on earth, He asked His disciples to learn to trust their Father in heaven and learn to stop worrying about things such as where they would sleep and what they would eat. Scripture tells us Jesus didn't have a home, or oftentimes a place to lay His head (Matthew 8:20). He and His disciples traveled for days at a time, going from town to town, sharing the good news that the Messiah was here.

On one occasion, Jesus sent his twelve disciples out to various towns without extra clothes, shoes, or food for their journey, asking them to completely trust their Father for their provisions. They had to learn how to be completely dependent on God for the basics of their survival – food and shelter.

"Therefore I tell you, do not be anxious about your life… Look at the birds of the air: they neither sow nor reap nor gather into

Ashley Djokoto

barns, and yet your heavenly Father feeds them. Are you not of more value than they? And which of you by being anxious can add a single hour to his span of life? And why are you anxious about clothing? Consider the lilies of the field, how they grow: they neither toil nor spin, yet I tell you, even Solomon in all his glory was not arrayed like one of these. But if God so clothes the grass of the field, which today is alive and tomorrow is thrown into the oven, will he not much more clothe you, O you of little faith?" Matthew 6:25-30

God asks the same of us today – Do we trust Him? Are we dependent on Him alone? The beautiful thing is that when we do put our trust in Him and stop worrying, we find out just how valuable we are to God. We are more valuable to God than any other part of creation He has created. He delights to give us good gifts and to provide for us (1 Timothy 6:17). He wants us to give our worries and cares to Him and rest in His perfect presence (1 Peter 5:7).

Challenge: What are you worried about? Are you anxious about something? Imagine giving that thing to God and releasing your hold on it. Spend time praying over the situation and asking for God to intervene.

Prayer: Lord, I thank You for valuing me so much more than You value the rest of your creation - the birds and animals, the streams and valleys. When I think of the beautiful scenery and the intricate processes of nature You have created, I wonder how You could value me above all the rest, but I know You do. Thank you. Please help me trust You more and more. I love You. Amen.

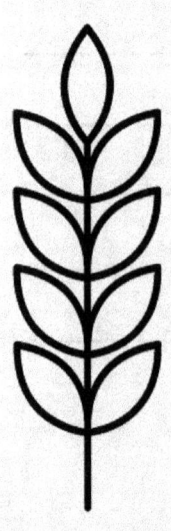

Part XVII

I am an overcomer

"For everyone who has been born of God overcomes the world. And this is the victory that has overcome the world—our faith. Who is it that overcomes the world except the one who believes that Jesus is the Son of God?"

1 John 5:4-5

I am an overcomer

"For everyone who has been born of God overcomes the world. And this is the victory that has overcome the world—our faith. Who is it that overcomes the world except the one who believes that Jesus is the Son of God?" 1 John 5:4-5

What is your greatest fear? One of mine is the fear of heights (which is ironic since I'm 6 foot 1). Fear has the capacity to incapacitate you. I once stood paralyzed on a 130-foot-high canopy walk through the trees of a national park in Ghana's Central Region. I literally could not move. I was grasping the tree as if my life depended on it, sure the rope bridge would break the minute my foot stepped off the ledge. My only choice was to go forward, though, as my friends tried to coax me onto the rough, wooden bridge, swaying in the breeze. I did, though terrified and crying the whole thousand feet to safety. I made it, eventually, to the other side and promised myself I would never do something like that again. I did, though, many years later and had many of the same fears and experiences. But I did it.

With Jesus' promise to work within us and around us, we are overcomers. Every fear, burden, shame, and bondage is broken in His Name. That does not necessarily mean those fears will leave, but it means we can walk through them and succeed despite them.

"I have said these things to you, that in me you may have peace. In the world you will have tribulation. But take heart; I have overcome the world." John 16:33

In every tribulation and trial, we are overcomers. Even in death, we have overcome because of Jesus' work on the cross. We no longer need to be afraid of death or anything else that may try to rob us of sleep at night. Through Christ, we are more than conquerors (Romans 8:37). So, whatever your fear is today, give it to Jesus, the author and perfecter of our faith, who will daily bear our burdens (Hebrews 12:2, Psalm 68:19).

Challenge: Write down those things that have you paralyzed. Maybe it is a fear or a secret sin you're afraid to tell anyone about. Then, take the paper and either burn it or tear it up and throw it away, symbolizing how it no longer has any hold on you. Pray through the scriptures in today's devotional and give your fears to the One who will help you overcome once and for all.

Prayer: Thank You, Jesus, for overcoming death on the cross for me. Thank You for making me an overcomer, too. Lord, I give You all my shame, fears, and things that have held me in bondage. Today, I throw them away and claim Your victory for me. Thank You. Help me live in victory today. I am an overcomer. I love You. Amen.

I am strong

"Wait for the LORD; be strong, and let your heart take courage; wait for the LORD!" Psalms 27:14

I am not a runner. I enjoy running, but I am not good at it, and I don't do it often. Once, I signed up to run a 5K, and just showed up on the day to run. I had not done the training or preparation required. I don't know what I was thinking. Somehow, I made it to the finish line, but I cannot tell you how I ran the entire way.

There are many other instances in my life where I cannot tell you how I made it through, except to say God gave me the strength. God often uses the tough, stressful circumstances in life to show us how much we need His strength to keep going. We cannot possibly do it on our own. Our human strength, intelligence, and grit are nowhere near enough. But thanks be to God – He is always sufficient, and He is always willing to give us more.

"Fear not, for I am with you; be not dismayed, for I am your God; I will strengthen you, I will help you, I will uphold you with my righteous right hand." Isaiah 41:10

For when those tough times come, and you don't know how you can keep going, God will give you the strength. It does not even make sense most of the time. Others may wonder how you do it. But somehow, one step at a time, you will make it through. And that is thanks to God's supernatural gift of strength.

"But they who wait for the LORD shall renew their strength; they shall mount up with wings like eagles; they shall run and not be weary; they shall walk and not faint." Isaiah 40:31

Challenge: Are you going through something stressful right now? Are you tired and feel like giving up? Pray and ask God for His supernatural strength. Spend time in worship and reading His Word. The more time we spend filling ourselves up with God's Presence, the more supernatural strength He will impart to us.

Prayer: God, thank You for supernatural strength. Thank You for never leaving me alone in the hard things. Please keep me at the center of Your will. Give me the strength to continue on this journey You have called me to. Let me never give up. Thank You for more strength. I love You. Amen.

I am full of endurance

"Blessed is the one who remains steadfast under trial, for when [she] has stood the test [she] will receive the crown of life, which God has promised to those who love Him."
James 1:12

Having endurance is hard. It is way easier to give up. Especially when the thing you are doing is difficult. Writing this devotional has taken me way longer than I had initially thought it would. So many times, I've nearly said, "Why bother?" I don't feel all that equipped or well-versed enough to write an actual book. Will it even get published? Am I wasting my time? Can God use me in this way? Will He? These questions have often caused me to stall in my writing. I've put it off, and then God convicts me to keep going. But still, it isn't easy to trust it will be worth it.

Can you relate? What are you struggling to finish? Have you been flirting with the idea of quitting because you can't see the worth? I encourage you to press on. There are so many people in the Bible who had to endure through some pretty difficult times. David knew he was the next king, but he spent years running from the current king and hiding in caves with next to nothing in his possession (1 Samuel 21-24). What kind of king has nothing to his name? Then there was Hannah, who was barren, crying for God to give her a baby (1 Samuel 1). Back then, if a woman was not married or had children, she was desolate. Or what about the woman with the issue of blood? We don't even know her name; we only know she had a medical debilitating disease for twelve years – She was shunned, ostracized, looked down upon, weakened physically and mentally, alone – for twelve years! Then, one day, she heard this man was healing people, and she decided to try it, though no other doctor had been able to heal her (Luke 8:43-48). And Jesus did. She merely touched His robe and was healed instantly.

"And let us not grow weary of doing good, for in due season we will reap a harvest if we do not give up." Galatians 6:9

It might seem like the road in front of you isn't worth walking, but I know from experience it is. No matter your circumstances, God is with you and will work them out for your good (Romans 8:28). That is His promise. All we have to do is continue in endurance.

Challenge: Choose one of the stories mentioned in today's devotional to read and meditate on: David, Hannah, or the woman with the issue of blood. Reflect on the challenges the person had and how they overcame those challenges. Reflect on the heartache and suffering they most likely experienced along the way. Ask yourself what benefits they received from not giving up. How did their stories end up influencing the entire generation?

Prayer: Thank You, Father, for Your unending provision and guidance. I know You have called me and purposed me for something special. Please help me endure. I can't understand why some things happen, but I know I can trust You. Please help me through. Please give me the strength and endurance to continue. I love You. Amen.

I am courageous

"Have I not commanded you? Be strong and courageous. Do not be frightened, and do not be dismayed, for the Lord your God is with you wherever you go." Joshua 1:9

One of my favorite places I have ever been is right here in Ghana. Wli Falls is the tallest waterfall in West Africa, and it is breathtaking. My friends and I decided to hike to the top a few years ago. It was supposed to take an average of six hours to hike the small mountain range to the top and then to the bottom of the falls. Little did we know we would be stuck in a thunderstorm along the way.

When we started, the welcome center sent a guide with us. When I saw him, I wasn't sure how helpful he could be, seeing as he was wearing flip-flops to hike a mountain! But we followed him, and he guided us up the mountain to the top of the falls. The view was amazing. On the way back down the mountain, however, it started pouring. Not only that, but the thunder and lightning were fierce! Here we were, following a guy wearing flip-flops down a muddy mountain, rain beating down on our heads through the trees. It's not something I ever want to experience again. It took us nine hours instead of the six we thought we had signed up for.

The whole way down, I was terrified. *God, what if I fall off this tiny ledge to my death? Why am I here? This is so not cool, God!* But with each step I took, I had no choice but to trust God would somehow get me to the bottom of the mountain or trust He would be with me if I did fall. That's the thing with God. He has promised to be with us and tells us repeatedly in His Word to take courage and take heart.

"Be strong and courageous. Do not fear or be in dread of them, for it is the Lord your God who goes with you. He will not leave you or forsake you." Deuteronomy 31:6

God will take you one step at a time. Courage is taking the step, even when you are scared and don't know what will happen when you do. As Nelson Mandela said, "Courage [is] not the absence of fear, but the triumph over it. The brave [woman] is not [she] who does not feel afraid, but [she] who conquers that fear."[25] For the woman with Christ in her corner, beating fear is much easier than for those without Him in their lives. We still feel afraid, but we have faith that God will work out His promises in our lives and is always working for our good and on our behalf (Romans 8:28). Having faith and being courageous go hand in hand, and both rely on a faithful and consistent God who loves us unconditionally.

Challenge: Choose a person from the Bible and read their story. Moses, Joshua, Peter, Paul, Esther, Mary, Rahab – the list goes on. Study their story and write down how that person showed faith amid fear. How did the person respond to their adversity with courage? Spend time asking God to help you show the same kind of courageousness in the face of your troubles. Ask Him to remind you daily that you can be courageous because He has you in the palm of His hand.

Ashley Djokoto

Prayer: Thank You, Father, for promising to never forsake me. Thank You for always taking care of me. Please help me trust You more. Please help me be courageous in this circumstance I'm facing. Help me respond to these troubles in faith instead of fear. I love You. Amen.

I am a conqueror

"Humble yourselves, therefore, under the mighty hand of God so that at the proper time he may exalt you, casting all your anxieties on him, because he cares for you. Be sober-minded; be watchful. Your adversary the devil prowls around like a roaring lion, seeking someone to devour. Resist him, firm in your faith, knowing that the same kinds of suffering are being experienced by your brotherhood throughout the world. And after you have suffered a little while, the God of all grace, who has called you to his eternal glory in Christ, will himself restore, confirm, strengthen, and establish you." 1 Peter 5:6-10

Life is hard. The more you grow up, the more and more you realize this to be true. Friends' betrayals, the loss of loved ones, the disappointments of not being chosen yet again – Every time life doesn't look like the way you planned it or dreamed it would be, it brings more realization that life is just plain hard.

When Jesus walked this earth incarnate, He suffered more than the typical Jewish man of that era. He not only was a subject under the Roman empire with the rest of his neighbors, meaning He had fewer rights and opportunities than a Roman citizen would, He also didn't have a stable home (Luke 9:58), was betrayed by two of his closest friends (Luke 22:58 and Luke 22:4), and was tortured in the most inhumanly way possible at that time.[26] If anyone had a hard life, it was Jesus. But the most crazy and amazingly wonderful thing is that He chose to live that life for you and me. If I could determine how my life story went, I would prefer a quiet and comfortable life surrounded by people I love. But Jesus knew He would face such horrors, and He chose to do it anyway – All to have a relationship with us. And now, thanks be to God, for He has provided a way for us to be conquerors in this life, too.

"But thank God! He gives us victory over sin and death through our Lord Jesus Christ." 1 Corinthians 15:57 (NIV)

So, the next time you are facing an overwhelming situation, remember Jesus has conquered, so you can, too. His power is so much more immense than we can ever really comprehend, and He's freely given it to you and me. So don't fear the temporary things this life may throw your way. Trust in Jesus – that He is leading you and will help you conquer any sin, disappointment, or difficulty.

Challenge: Read Romans 8:18-39. Which verses stand out to you? Pray the verses over your life and your mindset. Ask God to encourage you in whatever difficulty you may be facing now. Ask for courage and perseverance to continue this faith walk He has called you on as His daughter. Continue to sit and meditate on this passage as long as necessary.

Prayer: Jesus, thank You for going through all that pain and heartache for us. Thank You for conquering sin and death so I don't have to live in submission to them. Please help me conquer the sin in my life. Holy Spirit, do your work in me and help me persevere to the end. I love You. Amen.

Journal

Part XVIII

I am worth it

"Are not two sparrows sold for a penny? And not one of them will fall to the ground apart from your Father. But even the hairs of your head are all numbered. Fear not, therefore; you are of more value than many sparrows."

Matthew 10:29-31

I am worth it

"Are not two sparrows sold for a penny? And not one of them will fall to the ground apart from your Father. But even the hairs of your head are all numbered. Fear not, therefore; you are of more value than many sparrows." Matthew 10:29-31

Do you see yourself as worthy to God? A synonym for worthy is worthwhile. Do you see yourself as valuable? You are.

There is a story that Jesus tells his disciples about a shepherd who loses a sheep. All the others, the 99, are in the pen, but one goes missing. What would you do? To be honest, I think I would be like – good riddance – if the sheep is foolish enough to wander away into danger and fall off a cliff or be eaten by a wolf then he deserves his fate. But any good shepherd would find that one sheep. Any good shepherd would leave the other 99 sheep and walk many miles to find the one who wandered off.

I love the song "Reckless Love" [27] by Cory Ashbury because it echoes this fact and points us to Jesus, our Good Shepherd. It talks about how Jesus' love is so consuming that He would gladly not just leave the 99, but chase down the one. We cannot ever repay Him. We don't deserve it, but He died for us anyway. And when He was on that cross, His only thoughts were for you and me. That is why He stayed on that cross when He could have easily gotten down.

That is the way God's love is for us. He will leave the 99 to come after us when we go astray. He has for me, and He will for you. And we cannot ever repay Him. We don't deserve it, but He died for us anyway. And when He was on that cross, His only thoughts were for you and me. That is why He stayed on that cross when He could have easily gotten down.

Challenge: Look up *Reckless Love* and listen to the lyrics. Let them wash over you and meditate on your value to God.

Prayer: Thank You, Jesus, for dying for me. For choosing me and leaving the 99 to come after me. Thank You for saving me when You didn't have to. I can never repay You, and that's okay. Thank You for making a way when I couldn't. And all to have a relationship with me? It's amazing! I love You. Amen.

I am free

"For freedom Christ has set us free; stand firm therefore, and do not submit again to a yoke of slavery." Galatians 5:1

I think it's difficult for people to understand true freedom unless they have been under a yoke of bondage to someone or something. It is like someone who struggled with addiction for years but finally broke free. Or someone who fled from an oppressive society to finally find freedom in a new land. Most people will never go through such experiences, but all people begin their lives under the bondage of sin. The tricky thing is that most people will never realize this fact until something terrible or dramatic does happen.

Take my story, for instance. I've been a Christian almost my whole life, but in my young adult life, I got under the yoke of slavery again, as Galatians puts it, or in my case, the yoke of gossip. I did not realize my sin struggle was such a bondage until something horrible happened – all because of me and my choice to spread news that was not mine to share. At the time, I thought I was doing just fine, enjoying my friendships – besides, what could telling this secret to this friend hurt? We were all Christians, after all. But I did not realize that I only knew half the story, and when that rumor got back to my boss with my name attached to it – Let's say it was not my best moment. But it did wake me up that this small, harmless habit of gossiping with friends was not so harmless– and it was like a bondage over my life. I found this out the hard way when I tried to stop in my strength. But repeatedly, I heard myself say something and then regret it later. It's like I was not in control of my tongue (James 3:8). But thanks be to God, through prayer, submission, and lots of repentance, I can thankfully say I am no longer a slave to my sin.

"So if the Son sets you free, you will be free indeed." John 8:36

The fact was, I never really was a slave to that sin because of the work of Jesus on the cross, but I treated it like I was when I let it control me repeatedly instead of surrendering my weakness to my Savior and Redeemer. He has once and for all made us free from sin and death. Now, we can walk in freedom. But it is a mindset and a daily (or hourly) choice to do so. Will we stay stuck in our sin struggles and pretend they are not *that* bad, or will we humbly submit to our Father, who wants to help us grow away from those sins? The choice is ours, sisters, and I, for one, want to choose freedom.

Challenge: What is your sin struggle? What is one (or more) sin you are struggling with right now? Have you surrendered it to God, or are you trying to fix it on your own? Are you beating yourself up when you fail again, or are you letting yourself experience the grace that God pours on you? Spend time in prayer asking for forgiveness and God's strength to sanctify you in this way. Look up verses about forgiveness, grace, or freedom and meditate on them.

Prayer: Thank You, Lord, for Your never-ending forgiveness.

Ashley Djokoto

Thank You that I am no longer a slave to sin, but I have every victory over my sin because of You. Thank You for showing me how I must let go of my sin. Thank You for promising that You will walk with me and help me overcome sin. Please help me live for You. I love You. Amen.

I am sent

"Then Jesus came to them and said, 'All authority in heaven and on earth has been given to me. Therefore, go and make disciples of all nations, baptizing them in the name of the Father and of the Son and of the Holy Spirit, and teaching them to obey everything I have commanded you. And surely I am with you always, to the very end of the age.'" Matthew 28:18-20

I come from a long line of missionaries and travelers. My great-grandfather and great-grandmother migrated from Europe to America in the days of Ellis Island. My grandmothers left their homes to be missionaries. My parents grew up with the mindset that the world was meant to be explored and traveled, and they raised their children with the same attitude. When I was young, I wanted to be like the great missionaries like Elizabeth Elliot and Amy Carmichael. I wanted to go to the ends of the earth to share the gospel. After college, when I couldn't find anywhere to "go," I felt lost and unaccomplished. But through that time, I learned the importance of being sent is not in where you go or even what you do there, but in your humility of saying, "Here I am! Send me!" (Isaiah 6:8)

"But you will receive power when the Holy Spirit comes on you, and you will be my witnesses in Jerusalem, and in all Judea and

Ashley Djokoto

Samaria, and to the ends of the earth." Acts 1:8

This verse reminds me that we are to be His witnesses everywhere, not just "to the ends of the earth," as I believed when I was a child. It means in Judea, or your neighborhood. It is where you go to school and where you play sports, where you go to church and pick up your groceries. It means in Samaria, or your country. It means how you cast your vote or what you post about the injustices happening in your backyard. It means to the ends of the earth, or how much money you give to missions, or even how you give up a summer to serve on a short-term mission trip. You can be sent without ever leaving your nook of the world. It only depends on how willing you are to go.

When Isaiah wrote his famous words in Isaiah 6:8, "Here I am, send me," he wasn't aware he would be sent to a people who would despise him and the message he came to bring. He was not focused on who, what, where, and how. He was focused on the Holy Lamb of God sitting before Him, looking for someone to go for Him. And Isaiah was moved to say, "Yes, Lord, send me."

Are we moved in a similar way? I must admit, even living in another country than my own, there are some days when I am not. There are days I have heard the Holy Spirit telling me to go and share the good news by giving away this money or by saying a kind word, and instead, I retreat inside myself and stay in my comfortable cocoon. But that is not the way God wants us to live. He wants us to be bold and unashamed of the gospel (Romans 1:16). He wants us to accept the possible cost of going out of our comfort zone so that He can use us as His hands and feet to the broken and hurting people around us. And when we say, "Yes, Lord, send me, I'll go," I can promise it will be more than worth it. Even if you don't see a positive effect right away, you can be assured that God is working it out, and He has used you in a way you may never understand this side of heaven.

Challenge: Spend time praying for God to open your eyes to an opportunity to share the gospel today. I pray that He will give you a vision of a place or a person He wants you to go to or even a message He wants you to send. Once you hear from the Holy Spirit, don't delay. Often, in our waiting for "the perfect time," we end up talking ourselves out of it. After obeying, pray and ask God to use that word or kind gesture to bring that person or those persons closer to Him.

Prayer: Lord, I thank You that You want to send me. Thank You for speaking to me today. Please open my eyes to opportunities to share Your love with others no matter where I find myself. Please give me a boldness to share, even when I am scared. Help me, Lord. I want to obey You. I love You. Amen.

I am Victorious

"But thanks be to God, who gives us the victory through our Lord Jesus Christ. Therefore, my beloved brothers, be steadfast, immovable, always abounding in the work of the Lord, knowing that in the Lord your labor is not in vain."
1 Corinthians 15:57-58

There is nothing sweeter than the taste of victory after a long, hard battle. Interestingly enough, this is a scientific fact. Some researchers from Cornell University did a study with hockey players a few years ago.[28] They found that when given the same flavor of ice cream, the players' opinion of the product changed based on whether they had just won or lost their game. When they won, the ice cream was sweeter than when they lost. The researchers concluded that our taste buds could be tied to our mood. If that is the case, maybe going for ice cream after you break up with your boyfriend isn't a great idea. But the fact remains that victory after a long, hard battle is what every one of us craves.

David knew about long-suffering and battle. He waited years and years, hiding in the wilderness and even living with the enemy before he became King of Israel. And after he was finally named king, there was still no rest because he had to go into battle with the Philistines directly after. After one such war, it was noted that

"David danced before the Lord with all his might" (2 Samuel 6:14). He was so exceedingly happy about their victory, and not only for the victory over battle but also for the God who delighted to give it to them.

That same God gives us victory over our battles today. If you don't know, we are in a spiritual battle every day. The devil is looking for someone to devour and spread his lies and division everywhere he or his followers go, seeking ways to destroy God's kingdom and God's people. But God has given us the armor to stand and fight our enemy (Ephesians 6:10-20). Not only that, but He has promised He will help us and give us victory in the end.

"For everyone who has been born of God overcomes the world. And this is the victory that has overcome the world –our faith. Who is it that overcomes the world except the one who believes that Jesus is the Son of God?" 1 John 5:4-5

The only caveat for us overcoming and having victory is that we believe Jesus is God's Son. That is it. We don't have to be the strongest, bravest, or best Christian. We only need to put our hope in the One who is the most courageous, strongest, and best. That is the most relieving feeling in the world because I know on my own accord that I would not gain victory over my sin, let alone all the trials and tribulations this world brings us. But with God, we do have victory. We have victory to stand firm in our faith when others scoff at our expense, victory to persevere through the storms that come our way, and victory when we love others, especially when it is the most challenging thing to do. Ultimately, this victory will bring us to live with God forever in His Kingdom (Revelations 2:7).

Ashley Djokoto

Challenge: Read through Ephesians 6:10-20. Choose a commentary to read about these verses. Meditate on what the armor of God means practically for you. Draw the armor of God and list out prayers next to each armor of how you can put on this armor more readily in your life.

Prayer: Lord, I thank You for giving me victory over sin and death. Thank You for the sweet taste of victory. I ask that You give me victory over this sin and this challenge. Help me put on the full armor of God so I will be able to stand strong in my faith in You. I love You. Amen.

I am heaven-bound

"Behold, I stand at the door and knock. If anyone hears my voice and opens the door, I will come in to him and eat with him, and he with me. The one who conquers, I will grant him to sit with me on my throne, as I also conquered and sat down with my Father on His throne." Revelations 3:20-21

What is heaven like? I have wondered that more than a few times in my life. Will it be filled with white clouds and roads of gold and rubies? Will it be like our world, only cleaner and more perfect? Will we work, live, and play or stand before God and sing His praises 24-7? No one on this side of heaven knows what heaven will be like. But what we do know is that it will be perfect.

Right before Jesus went to the place where He knew He would die, He comforted His disciples with the fact that they would get to come to the place He where He was going to go - heaven. Why do you think He wanted to make sure his friends knew this before He left them? Don't you think they would have been terrified that they would be next? After all, we see the disciples were so afraid that they ran away (one even leaving naked to get away), and Peter was so scared to be seen with Jesus that he denied Him not once, but three times (Mark 14:52 and Matthew 26:69-75). Jesus knew this was coming, so He wanted them to be able to recall what He

Ashley Djokoto

had previously said about heaven.

"Let not your hearts be troubled. Believe in God; believe also in me. In my Father's house are many rooms. If it were not so, would I have told you that I go to prepare a place for you? And if I go and prepare a place for you, I will come again and will take you to myself, that where I am you may be also." John 14:1-3

He also wants us to be reminded that Jesus has prepared a place for us with Him in Heaven. He has a room already set up for you and me. The best news yet is that when Jesus returns, there will be no more suffering, pain, or tears (Revelation 21:4), and all things will be completely restored to perfection, like how it was before sin entered the world. This is what our souls are longing for – a perfected relationship with the One who created us and loves us.

Challenge: Read Revelations 21, the second to last chapter in the Bible, about the New Heaven and Earth. When Jesus returns a second time, He will create a new heaven and earth where His people reside with Him forever. It will be like the perfect Garden of Eden - everything is restored to their former glory. Sit for a minute and imagine what that will be like. Spend time thanking God for this marvelous truth - that He has prepared a way for us to be with Him forever in this amazing place of His glory.

Prayer: Thank You, Lord Jesus, for preparing for us a place to live and commune with You for all eternity. How can I ever thank You enough for not giving us what we deserve - punishment and death—and instead giving us grace and forgiveness? Not only that but a new life and a future life with You. I love You, and I cannot wait for You to return. Come, Lord Jesus, come! Amen.

Journal

About Author

A dedicated educator and wife with a deep passion for mentoring young women, Ashley Djokoto has spent the last fifteen years making a meaningful impact through teaching and mentoring. Her dedication to young women extends beyond the classroom, evident in her published devotions featured on platforms like Velvet Ashes, The Devoted Collective, and Milk and Honey Books.

With a genuine love for reading and deep conversations with friends, she invites readers to join her on a journey of faith, identity, and purpose. Explore the complexities of life alongside her as she shares insights drawn from a life devoted to serving Jesus. Though her first home is in Georgia, her second home in Ghana is where she resides with her amazing husband and her adorable dog.

Endnotes

1. Gaultiere, Bill, et al. "Biblical Meditation: Using Imagination to Pray." Soul Shepherding - Following Jesus for Deeper Life and Greater Influence., 15 Dec. 2023, www.soulshepherding.org/biblical-meditation-using-imagination-pray.Nierenberg, Cari. "Having a Baby: Stages of

2. Pregnancy." Live Science, Live Science, 30 Aug. 2017, www.livescience.com/44899-stages-of-pregnancy.html.Siegel, Ethan. "Ask Ethan: Could You Have Two Perfectly Identical

3. Snowflakes?" Forbes, www.forbes.com/sites/startswithabang/2017/01/14/ask-ethan-could-you-have-two-perfectly-identical-snowflakes/?sh=23f9ba6944e4. Accessed 2 Jan. 2024."How Many

4. Languages Are in the World Today? - Swap Language Blog." Swap Language Blog, 18 Jan. 2022, swaplanguage.com/blog/how-many-languages-in-the-world/#:~:text=With%20%E2%80%9Conly%E2%80%9D%20195%20countries%20in."A Revealing Map of the World's Most and Least

5. Ethnically Diverse Countries." Washington Post, 1 Dec. 2021, www.washingtonpost.com/news/worldviews/wp/2013/05/16/a-revealing-map-of-the-worlds-most-and-least-ethnically-diverse-countries/#:~:text=Because%20data%20sources%20such%20as. Accessed 2 Jan. 2024.

6. "Skin Pigmentation | AncestryDNA® Traits Learning Hub." Www.ancestry.com, www.ancestry.com/c/traits-learning-hub/skin-pigmentation#:~:text=From%20pale%20to%20dark%20and.

7. "Hematidrosis (Sweating Blood): Causes and Treatment." Healthline, 14 Mar. 2017, www.healthline.com/health/hematidrosis#:~:text=Hematidrosis%20is%20an%20extremely%20rare. Accessed 3 Jan. 2024.

8. The Veil of the Tabernacle | Christian Library. www.christianstudylibrary.org/article/veil-tabernacle.
9. Lyons, Josh. "Medical Evidence Supports Biblical Instruction: Don't Eat Pork." Tomorrow's World, 13 June 2023, www.tomorrowsworld.org/commentary/medical-evidence-supports-biblical-instruction-dont-eat-pork. Accessed 3 Jan. 2024.
10. "How Do Oysters Make Pearls?" Natural History Museum, www.nhm.ac.uk/discover/quick-questions/how-do-oysters-make-pearls.html#:~:text=Pearls%20are%20made%20by%20marine,also%20make%20up%20its%20shell.
11. "Hymn: Turn Your Eyes upon Jesus." Www.hymnal.net, www.hymnal.net/en/hymn/h/645.
12. "The Simple Art of Grafting Fruit Trees: A Complete Guide." Orchard People, 6 June 2023, orchardpeople.com/grafting-fruit-trees/.
13. "Definition of ANOINT." Www.merriam-Webster.com, 23 Dec. 2023, www.merriam-webster.com/dictionary/anoint#:~:text=%3A%20to%20smear%20or%20rub%20with. Accessed 3 Jan. 2024.
14. https://www.facebook.com/JohnPiper. "You Are Anointed: How the Truth Becomes Precious." Desiring God, 18 Nov. 2018, www.desiringgod.org/messages/you-are-anointed.
15. "Sunrise and Sunset Times in Jerusalem." Timeanddate.com, 2020, www.timeanddate.com/sun/israel/jerusalem.
16. "He Will Hold Me Fast." Hymnary.org, hymnary.org/text/when_i_fear_my_faith_will_fail. Accessed 3 Jan. 2024.
17. "Number of Species on Earth - Current Results." Currentresults.com, 2014, www.currentresults.com/Environment-Facts/Plants-Animals/number-species.php.
18. Watson, Traci. "86 Percent of Earth's Species Still Unknown?" Science, 25 Aug. 2011, www.nationalgeographic.com/science/article/110824-earths-species-8-7-million-biology-planet-animals-science.
19. Poor, Jeffery Curtis. The True Meaning of Helpmate (4 Powerful Truths from Genesis 2:18). 7 June 2021, www.rethinknow.org/helpmate-ezer-meaning/. Accessed 3 Jan. 2024.

20. "Broken Toe: Symptoms, Recovery, and More." Healthline, 5 May 2023, www.healthline.com/health/broken-toe#_noHeaderPrefixedContent. Accessed 3 Jan. 2024.

21. Shore, Summer. You Are God's Beloved – Experience Revival. experiencerevival.com/2019/01/30/beloved/.

22. "Turkish Churches Stress Unity amid Quake Devastation as Christians Supply Aid to Rebuild." CBN, 23 Feb. 2023, www2.cbn.com/news/israel/turkish-churches-stress-unity-amid-quake-devastation-christians-supply-aid-rebuild. Accessed 3 Jan. 2024.

23. Harris, Hamil R. "Churches Offer Hope, Support after Devastating Mississippi Tornadoes." The Washington Informer, 3 May 2023, www.washingtoninformer.com/churches-offer-hope-support-after-devastating-mississippi-tornadoes/. Accessed 3 Jan. 2024.

24. Why Do Young Women Have Such Low Self-Esteem? | Amen Clinics Amen Clinics. www.amenclinics.com/blog/why-do-young-women-have-such-low-self-esteem.

25. McKenna, Amy. "Nelson Mandela Quotes | Britannica." Encyclopædia Britannica, 2019, www.britannica.com/list/nelson-mandela-quotes.

26. Retief, F. P., and L. Cilliers. "The History and Pathology of Crucifixion." South African Medical Journal = Suid-Afrikaanse Tydskrif Vir Geneeskunde, vol. 93, no. 12, 1 Dec. 2003, pp. 938–941, pubmed.ncbi.nlm.nih.gov/14750495/#:~:text=In%20antiquity%20crucifixion%20was%20considered.

27. "Cory Asbury - Reckless Love Lyrics | AZLyrics.com." Www.azlyrics.com, www.azlyrics.com/lyrics/coryasbury/recklesslove.html. (need actual permission, not just citing)

28. "Just How Sweet Is the Taste of Victory?" NPR.org, www.npr.org/2015/09/06/438008983/just-how-sweet-is-the-taste-of-victory.

www.ingramcontent.com/pod-product-compliance
Lightning Source LLC
Chambersburg PA
CBHW070131080526
44586CB00015B/1651